CONTENTS OF VOLUME TWO

The Arts and Crafts of Older Spain

(Volume II)

Leonard Williams

Alpha Editions

This edition published in 2020

ISBN : 9789354022289

Design and Setting By
Alpha Editions
email - alphaedis@gmail.com

THE
ARTS AND CRAFTS OF
OLDER SPAIN

BY

LEONARD WILLIAMS

COMENDADOR OF THE ORDER OF ALFONSO THE TWELFTH

CORRESPONDING MEMBER OF THE ROYAL SPANISH ACADEMY;
OF THE ROYAL SPANISH ACADEMY OF HISTORY; AND
OF THE ROYAL SPANISH ACADEMY OF FINE ARTS

AUTHOR OF "THE LAND OF THE DONS";
"TOLEDO AND MADRID"; "GRANADA," ETC.

*VOLUME
TWO*

T. N. FOULIS, 23 BEDFORD STREET,
LONDON, W.C.; & 13-15 FREDERICK
STREET, EDINBURGH . . . MDCCCCVII.

LIST OF ILLUSTRATIONS

VOLUME TWO

FURNITURE

LIST OF ILLUSTRATIONS

LIST OF ILLUSTRATIONS

LIST OF ILLUSTRATIONS

Furniture

FURNITURE

WHETHER the primitive Iberians ate as well as slept upon their cave or cabin floor, or whether—as some classics call upon us to believe—they used a kind of folding-chair (*dureta*) and (more advanced and comfort-loving than the Andalusian rustics of this day) devoured their simple meal from benches or supports constructed in the wall, is not of paramount importance to the history of Spanish furniture. The statements of those early authors may be granted or rejected as we please; for not a single piece of furniture produced by prehistoric, or, indeed, by Roman or by Visigothic Spain, has been preserved. But if we look for evidence to other crafts, recovered specimens of her early gold and silver work and pottery show us that Roman Spain grew to be eminently Roman in her social and artistic life. This fact, together with the statements of Saint Isidore and certain other writers of his day, would seem to prove that all the usual articles of Roman furniture were commonly adopted by the subjugated tribes, and subsequently by the Visigoths;—the Roman eating-couch or *lectus triclinaris*, the state-bed or *lectus genialis*, the ordinary sleeping-bed or *lectus cubicularis*, made, in prosperous households, of luxurious woods inlaid with ivory, or even of gold and silver; lamps or candelabra of silver, copper, glass, and iron[1]; the *cathedra* or chair for women, the *bisellium* or seat for honoured guests, the *solium* or chair for the head of the house, the simpler chairs without a back, known as the *scabellum* and the *sella*, and the benches or *subsellia* for the servants. Further, the walls were hung with tapestries or rendered cheerful by mural painting; while the fireplace[2] and the brasier (*foculus*) have descended to contemporary Spain.

[1] Documents, quoted by the Count of Clonard, of Alfonso the Second, San Genadio, Froylan, and the Infanta Urraca.

[2] According to Miquel y Badía, the *focus* of the Romans is the present *clar de foch* of Cataluña; "a square platform of brick or stone raised somewhat from the ground, surrounded by a bench (*escó*), and large enough to serve for roasting beasts entire."

Swinburne wrote from Reus in 1775;—"we here for the first time saw a true Spanish kitchen, viz., an hearth raised above the level of the floor under a wide funnel, where a circle of muleteers were huddled together over a few cinders."

FURNITURE

Advancing to a period well within the reach of history, we find that early in the Middle Ages Spain's seigniorial mansions and the houses of the well-to-do were furnished in a style of rude magnificence. Roman models, derived from purely Roman and Byzantine sources through the Visigoths, continued to remain in vogue until the tenth or the eleventh century.[1] Then, as the fashion of these declined, the furniture of Christian Spain was modified in turn by Moorish, Gothic, and Renaissance art ; or two of these would overlap and interact, or even all the three.

During the Middle Ages the furniture of the eating, sleeping, and living room which formed the principal apartment in the mansion of a great seignior, was very much the same throughout the whole of Christian Europe. Viollet-le-Duc has described it in the closest detail. The dominant object, looming in a corner, was the ponderous bed, transformed into a thing of beauty by its costly

[1] The *Codex of the Testaments*, preserved in Oviedo Cathedral, contains some valuable illustrations of Spanish furniture of the tenth century. Greatly interesting, too, is the chair of San Raimundo (12th century) preserved at Roda in Aragon. It is of the "scissors" or folding form (*sella plicatilis*, Ducange), and the arms are terminated by heads of animals.

3

canopy and hangings.[1] Throughout the earlier mediæval times the Spanish bedstead was of iron or bronze. Wood, plain at first, then richly carved, succeeded metal towards the fourteenth century, and with this change the bed grew even vaster than before. Often it rose so high above the level of the flooring that the lord and lady required a set of steps to clamber up to it. These steps were portable, and sometimes made of solid silver.[2] I quote herewith a full description of a mediæval

[1] The early nomenclature of the clothes and other fittings of a Spanish bed is bewildering. We find in common use the canopy (*almocalla, almuzala*; Arabic, *al-mokalla*, i.e. "haven of refuge in all winds"—not always, possibly, a judicious term in the case of a *cama de matrimonio* or "marriage-bed"); the cloth-lined skins for chilly weather (*alifafe, alifad*; Arabic *al-lifafh*), such as King Juan the First of Aragon provided for his daughter ("two leathers of Morocco for the bed." *Archive of the Crown of Aragon; Registro* 1906, *fol.* 42); the parament or *dosal*; the *galnapé* or topmost of the bedclothes proper ("*un lecho con guenabe*"; Fuero of Cáceres, A.D. 1229); the counterpane (*fatel, fatol, alfatel, facel, farele, fateye, fatiro*; Arabic *fatla*); the linen sheets (*izares, lentros, lentos, lintes, lincas, linteáminas,* or *lencios*); and the mattress, pillow, and bolster, called, all three of them, *plumazo, plumario,* or *plumaco.* Nearly or quite identical in meaning with these last are *cúlcita* and *almadraque. Cúlcita* is corrupted into *colcedra, cocedra, conzara, colotra,* and other more or less barbaric variations; while *almohada, almuella, travesera, almofadinha, faseruelo,* and *aljamar* also signify a pillow or a cushion.

[2] "E due haber encara héla entegrament, ses vestitz é ses joyes é un leyt ben garnit del misllors apereylltz que sien en casa, é *una*

4

FURNITURE

Spanish bed, extracted from an inventory of the Princess Juana which was made upon her marriage with the Count of Foix, in 1392. The same bed had formerly belonged to Juana's mother, the Princess Martha, at her marriage with King Juan the First. It had "a velvet canopy with lions of gold thread, and a dove and a horse confronting every lion. And each of the lions and doves and horses bears a lettering; and the lettering of the lions is *Estre por voyr*, and that of the doves and horses *aay*, and the whole is lined with green cloth. *Item*, a counterpane of the said velvet, with a similar design of doves and lions, and likewise lined with green cloth. *Item*, three curtain-pieces of fine blue silk, with their metal rings and cords of blue thread. *Item*, three cushion-covers of blue velvet, two of them of large size, bearing two lions on either side, and four of them small, with a single lion on either side, embroidered with gold thread; with their linen coverings. *Item*, a cloth of a barred pattern, with the bars of blue velvet and cloth of gold upon a red ground; which cloth serves for a state-chair or for a window, and is lined with cloth. *Item*,

escala d'argent é una cortina." Fuero of Jaca, A.D. 1331, quoted by Abad y la Sierra and the Count of Clonard.

5

another cloth made of the said velvet and cloth of gold, which serves for the small chair (*reclinatorio*) for hearing Mass, and is lined with the aforesaid green cloth. *Item*, two large linen sheets enveloping the aforesaid canopy and counterpane. A pair of linen sheets, of four breadths apiece, bordered on every side with a handbreadth of silk and gold thread decoration consisting of various kinds of birds, leaves, and letters ; and each of the said sheets contains at the head-end about five handbreadths of the said decoration. *Item*, four cushions of the same linen, all of them adorned all round with about a handbreadth of the aforesaid decoration of birds, leaves, and letters. *Item*, two leather boxes, lined with wool, which contained all these objects. *Item*, five canvas-covered cushions stuffed with feather, for use with the said six coverings of blue velvet bearing the said devices. *Item*, three large pieces of wall tapestry made of blue wool with the same devices of lions, horses, and doves, made likewise of wool, yellow and of other colours. *Item*, five carpets made of the aforesaid wool, bearing the same devices. *Item*, three coverlets of the same wool, and with the same devices, for placing on the bed. *Item*, a coverlet of red leather bearing in its centre the

6

FURNITURE

arms of the King and the Infanta. *Item*, another coverlet made of leather bars and plain red leather. *Item*, a woollen coverlet with the arms of the Infanta." [1]

Another corner of the room was occupied by the dining-table,[2] spread at meal-times with a cloth denominated by Saint Isidore the *mappa*, *mápula*, *mapil*, *mantella*, or *mantellha*; and laid with the *mandíbulas* or "jaw-wipers" (*i.e.* napkins; see Du Cange), plates (*discos*), dishes (*mensorios*, *messorios*, or *misorios*), spoons (*cocleares*, *culiares*), though not as yet with forks,[3] cups of various shapes and substances, with or without a cover (*copos*, *vásculos*, and many other terms), the water-flagon (*kana*, *mikana*, *almakana*), the cruet-stand (*canatella*), and the salt-cellar (*salare*).

This table also served to write upon, while in its neighbourhood would stand the massive side-

[1] Sanpere y Miquel; *Las costumbres catalanas en tiempo de Juan* I., pp. 83, 84.

[2] Miquel y Badía believes that the Spaniards abandoned the Roman usage of reclining at their meals towards the sixth century.

[3] Forks were not introduced till later. It has even been questioned whether they were known in Spain as late as the sixteenth century. But Ambrosio de Morales mentions one in 1591, while another is recorded in 1607 as belonging to the monastery of San Jerónimo de Valparaiso, near Cordova. (See vol. i., p. 84.)

board, piled with gold and silver plate, and vessels of glass or ivory, wood or alabaster.

Besides the bed and table in their several corners, the chamber would contain a suitable variety of chairs and stools, mostly surrounding the capacious fireplace. Members of the household also sat on carpets spread upon the floor. The great arm-chair of the seignior himself was more ornate than any of the rest, and was provided somewhat later with a lofty Gothic back (Plates i. and ii.). A chair with a back of moderate height was destined for distinguished visitors. The back of ordinary chairs reached only to about the sitter's shoulder, and coverings of cloth or other stuffs were not made fast, but hung quite loosely from the wooden frame. This usage lasted till the sixteenth century, when the upholsterers began to nail the coverings of the larger chairs and benches.

Owing to the oriental influence brought back from the Crusades, the furniture of Europe, not excluding Spain, grew ever more elaborate and costly, while further, in the case of this Peninsula, the native Moorish influence operated steadily and strongly from Toledo, Seville, Cordova, Valencia, and elsewhere. Tapestries of Eastern manufacture (*alcatifas*) were now in general use for decorating

FURNITURE

floors and walls. The bed grew more and more
gigantic, and its clothes and curtains more extrava-
gantly sumptuous, until the florid Gothic woodwork harmonized with canopies and curtains cut
from priceless skins, or wrought in gold and silver
thread on multicolor satin and brocade. And at
the bed's head, like some jewel marvellously set,
rested, in every noble home, the diptych or the
triptych with its image of the Saviour or the
Virgin Mary.

Under the influence of the Renaissance this
love of luxury continued to increase among the
royal and the noble families of Spain. In 1574 an
inventory of the estate of Doña Juana, sister of
Philip the Second, mentions a silver balustrade,
weighing one hundred and twenty-one pounds,
for placing round a bed. The inventory (1560)
of the Dukes of Alburquerque contains a great
variety of entries relative to the furniture and
chamber-fittings of the period. We find here
mentioned, Turkey carpets and the celebrated
Spanish ones of Alcaraz, linens of Rouen, green
cloth of Cuenca, Toledo cloths, hangings of Arras
and elsewhere, tablecovers of damask and of
velvet, gold-fringed canopies (*doseles*) of green or
crimson velvet or brocade, a "canopy for a side-

board, of red and yellow Toledo cloth, with the arms of the La Cuevas in embroidery, together with stripes and bows, and repetitions of the letter I (for *Isabel Giron*, the duchess), also embroidered fringes of the same cloth, and cords of the aforesaid colours." We also read of a *sitial* or statechair of crimson satin brocade, and "a small walnut table covered with silver plates, bearing the arms of my lord the duke and of my lady the duchess, and edged with silver stripes."[1] The bedstead, fitted with hangings of double taffeta and scarlet cloth, was no less sumptuous than the other objects.

A popular and even an indispensable piece of furniture in every mediæval Spanish household was the *caja de novia* or "bride's chest." The use of this, as well as of a smaller kind of box, was common both to Moors and Christians. No matter of what size, these objects were essentially the same. They served innumerable purposes;

[1] This kind of furniture was prohibited by a sumptuary pragmatic of 1594. "No silversmith or other craftsman, or any person whatsoever, shall make, or cause to be made, or sold, or sell himself or purchase, whether openly or privately, buffets, writing-desks, chests, brasiers, pattens, tables, letter-cases, *rejillas* or foot-warmers, images, or any other object that has silver fittings, whether the silver be beaten, stamped, wrought in relief, carved, or plain." *Suma de todas las leyes* (A.D. 1628), p. 42.

MEDIÆVAL CHAIR

(Carved with the arms of Castile and Leon)

FURNITURE

were made of all dimensions—from the tiniest casket (*arcellina, capsula,* or *pyxide*; see vol. i., p. 45 *et seq.*) to the ponderous and vast *arcón,*—and almost any substance — ivory or crystal, mother-of-pearl or glass, gold, silver, copper, silver-gilt, jasper, agate, or fine wood; and we find them in every part of the Peninsula, from the dawn of the Middle Ages till very nearly the end of the eighteenth century.

According to the Marquis of Monistrol, the larger boxes or *arcones* constitute by far the commonest article of Spanish furniture all through the earlier portion of this lengthy period. The same authority divides them broadly into seven classes, thus :—

(1) Burial-chests.
(2) Chests for storing chasubles, chalices, candelabra, and other objects connected with the ceremonies of the church.
(3) Archive-chests, for storing documents.
(4) Chests for storing treasure (*huches*).
(5) Brides' chests.
(6) Chests for storing arms.
(7) *Arcones - trojes,* or chests of common make, employed for storing grain in country dwellings or *posadas.*

ARTS AND CRAFTS OF OLDER SPAIN

The decorative richness of these quaint *arcones* varies according to their date of manufacture, or the purpose they were meant to serve. Commonly, in the earliest of them, dating from the sixth or seventh century, the iron clamps or fastenings form the principal or only ornament. Such are reported to have been the two chests which the Cid Campeador loaded with sand and foisted as filled with specie on his "dear friends" Rachel and Vidas, the Jewish though trustful usurers of Burgos, in return for six hundred marks of gold and silver. Tradition says, moreover, that the chest now shown at Burgos as the "coffer of the Cid" is actually one of these. It is certain that the archives of the cathedral have been deposited in this chest for many centuries. Evidently, too, it dates from about the lifetime of the Cid, while the rings with which it is fitted show it to have been a kind of trunk intended to be carried on the backs of sumpter-mules or horses.

After the Roman domination in this country, the Latin term *capsa* was applied to every kind of chest ; but at a later age sepulchral chests or coffins were denominated *urns*, in order to distinguish them from *arcas* and *arcones*, which were used for storing clothes or jewellery. Excellent examples

12

GOTHIC CHAIR

(15th Century)

FURNITURE

of Spanish mediæval burial-chests are those of
Doña Urraca, preserved in the Sagrario of the
cathedral of Palencia, and of San Isidro, patron
of Madrid. The former, mentioned by painstak-
ing Ponz, and by Pulgar in his *Secular and
Ecclesiastical Annals of Palencia*, is of a plain
design, and really constitutes a coffin. The sepulchral chest of San Isidro, dating from the end of
the thirteenth century, or the early part of the
fourteenth, and kept at Madrid in a niche of the
camarín of the parish church of San Andrés, is
in the Romanic style, and measures seven feet
six inches in length. It has a gable top, and is
painted in brilliant colours on plaster-coated
parchment, with miracles effected by the saint,
and other scenes related with his life ; but much
of the painting is effaced.

Another interesting sepulchral chest would
probably have been the one presented in 1052
by Ferdinand the First, together with his royal
robe and crown,[1] to the basilica of Saint John
the Baptist at León, to guard the remains of

---

[1] Describing how the monarch made these presents to the church
when lying at the point of death, the *Chronicle of the Monk of Silos*
says : "*exuit regalem clamydem, qua induebatur corpus et deposuit
gemmatam coronam, qua ambiebatur caput.*"

ARTS AND CRAFTS OF OLDER SPAIN

Saint Isidore.   This chest was covered with thick
gold plates studded with precious stones, and
bore, in enamel and relief, the figures of the
apostles gathered round the Saviour, and medallions containing figures of the Virgin, saints, and
martyrs.   According to Ambrosio de Morales,
the gold plates were torn off by Alfonso the
First of Aragon, who replaced them by others
of silver-gilt.   The same monarch, regardless of
the church's fierce anathema pronounced on all
who dared to touch her property,[1] is accused by
his chronicler of having appropriated a box of
pure gold studded with gems, enshrining a crucifix
made of the true Cross, and which was kept in
some town or village of the kingdom of León.
Doubtless as a chastisement for Alfonso's impiety,
this precious box was captured from him by the
Moors at the battle of Fraga.

Among the reliquary chests, the oldest specimen
extant in Spain is the *arca santa* of Oviedo
cathedral.   This object, which is purely Byzantine
in its style, is believed to have been made at

[1] The formula is worded thus : " *Quisquis ille fuerit qui talia
commiserit, sit maledictus coram Deo et Angelis ejus, mendicitas
et lepra prosapiam teneat suam et extraneus persistat a sancta
communione, quatenus cum Juda, Christi proditore, ardendus per-
maneat in æterna damnatione.*"

FURNITURE

Constantinople. It was improved by Alfonso the Sixth, who added *repoussé* plates to it, with Arabic ornamentation in the form of meaningless inscriptions of a merely decorative character, but which are interesting as showing the kinship existing at this time between the Spanish Christians and the Spanish Moors.

Equally important is the coffer which was made by order of Don Sancho el Mayor to enshrine the wonder-working bones of San Millan, and which is now at San Millan de la Cogulla, in the province of La Rioja. The author of this chest, which dates from A.D. 1033, is vaguely spoken of as "Master Aparicio." The chest itself consists of a wooden body beneath a covering of ivory and gold, further enriched with statuettes and studded with real and imitation stones. It is divided into twenty-two compartments carved in ivory with passages from the life and miracles of the saint, and figures of "princes, monks, and benefactors," who had contributed in one way or another to the execution of the reliquary.

I have said that the "coffer of the Cid" was made for carrying baggage. A very interesting Spanish baggage-chest, although more modern than the Cid's by several centuries, is now the property of Señor Moreno Carbonero (Plate iii.). This very competent authority believes it to have belonged to Isabella the Catholic, and says that it was formerly the usage of the sovereigns of this country to mark their baggage-boxes with the first quartering of the royal arms and also with their monogram. Such is the decoration, consisting of repeated castles and the letter Y (for Ysabel), upon this trunk. The space between is painted red upon a surface thinly spread with wax. Strips of iron, twisted to imitate the girdle of Saint Francis, are carried over all the frame, surrounding the castles and the letters. This box was found at Ronda.[1]

A handsome *arcón*, dating from the same period as this baggage-chest of Isabella the Catholic, namely, the end of the fifteenth century, is stated by its owner, Don Manuel Lopez de Ayala, to

[1] To keep the dust or rain from entering these trunks, they were covered, when on the march, with stout square cloths called *reposteros*, which were often richly worked and bore the owner's arms or monogram. The same word subsequently came to mean the tapestried or other decorative cloths displayed in Spain on gala days from balconies of public edifices, or the mansions of the aristocracy ; but dictionaries which were printed at the close of the eighteenth century still define the *repostero* as "caparison, a square cloth with the arms of a prince or lord on it, which serves to cover a led-horse, or sumpter-horse."

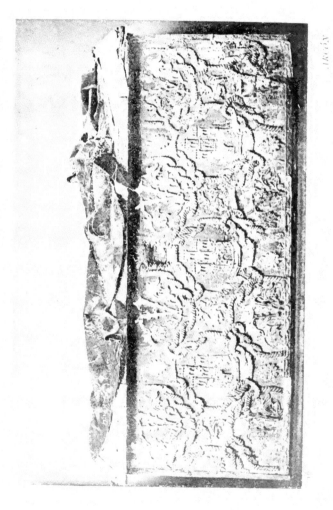

III

FURNITURE

have belonged to Cardinal Cisneros (Plate iv.).
The material is wood, covered inside with dark
blue cloth, and outside with red velvet, most of
the nap of which is worn away. The dimensions
are four feet six inches in length, two feet in
height, and twenty inches in depth. The chest,
which has a triple lock, is covered with *repoussé*
iron plates representing twisted columns and
other architectural devices, combined with Gothic
thistle-leaves. A coat of arms is on the front.

Such is an outline of the history of these
Spanish chests. Most of the earlier ones are
cumbersome and scantily adorned. Then, as
time proceeds, we find on them the florid Gothic
carving, unsurpassed for purity and charm; then
the Renaissance, with its characteristic ornament of
urns, and birds, and intertwining frond and ribbon;
and finally, towards, and lasting through the
greater portion of, the eighteenth century, the
tasteless and decadent manner of Baroque. Yet
even in the worst and latest we descry from time
to time a flickering remnant of the art of Moorish
Spain.

These Spanish Moors, obedient to the custom
of their fellow-Mussulmans throughout the world,
employed but little furniture. They loved, indeed,

bright colours and ingenious craftsmanship, but rather in the adjuncts to their furniture than in the furniture itself; in costly carpets, or worked and coloured leather hung upon the wall,[1] or spread upon their *alhamíes* and *alhanías*; in fountains bubbling in the middle of their courts and halls; in doors, and ceilings, and *celosías* exquisitely carved, and joined with matchless cunning; in flower-vases placed in niches; in bronze or silver perfume-burners rolling at their feet; but not (within the ordinary limit of the term) in furniture. Upon this theme the Reverend Lancelot Addison discourses very quaintly. "The host here," he wrote of "West Barbary" in 1663, "is one Cidi Caffian Shat, a grandee, reported to be an An-

[1] The wood-carving and decorative leather-work of older Spain will be described a little later on. As to the use of decorated leather by the Moors, in the small chamber of the Alhambra opening into the Mirador of Daraxa, and known as the Sala de los Ajimeces, is a bare space about nine feet in height, which runs the whole way round beneath the copious ornament of the remainder of the wall. Contreras says that the Moorish sultans used to hang these spaces with decorated leathers, tapestry, and armour. Sometimes the tapestry or leather would be worked or painted with hunting-scenes (*tardwahsh*—the chase of the lion, panther, or wild boar), or even with portraits of the sultans. Among these latter is the celebrated painting on the ceiling of the Hall of Justice, executed, as are its companions at each side of it, upon a leather groundwork with a plaster coating.

IV

ARCA OF CARDINAL CISNEROS

FURNITURE

dalusian, one of the race of the Moors bansht (*sic*)
Spain. . . . . We were called to a little upper
Room, which we could not enter till we had put
off our shoes at the threshold : not for Religion,
but Cleanliness, and not to prevent our unhal-
lowing the floor, but defiling the carpets wherewith
it was curiously spread. At the upper end of the
Room was laid a Velvit Cushion, as large as
those we use in our Pulpits, and it denoted the
most Honourable part of the Room. After we
had reposed about an hour, there was brought in
a little oval Table, about twenty Inches high, which
was covered with a long piece of narrow linnen ;
and this served for Diaper.[1] For the Moors, by
their law, are forbidden such superfluous Utensils
as napkins, knives, spoons, etc. Their Religion
laying down the general maxim, that meer
necessaries are to be provided for ; which caused
a precise Moor to refuse to drink out of my dish

---

[1] I think this shows why to this day a Spaniard who professes to
be an educated person will often wipe his or her mouth upon the
tablecloth. Not many weeks ago I saw the elegantly dressed
daughter of a Spanish member of Parliament perform this semi-
oriental feat in an hotel at Granada. Montaigne would judge this
señorita with benevolence ; not so, I fear, my compatriots. Similarly, it is considered rude in Spain to stretch yourself ; but not to
spit upon the dining-room floor, or pick your teeth at table.

when he could sup water enough out of the hollow of his hand."

The same author proceeds to relate his experiences at bed-time. " Having supp'd and solaced ourselves with muddy beverage and Moresco music, we all composed ourselves to sleep : about twenty were allotted to lodge in this small chamber, whereof two were Christians, three Jews, and the rest Moors ; every one made his bed of what he wore, which made our English constitutions to wish for the morning."

Among the Mussulmans all this has undergone no change. Do we not find their present furniture to be identical with that of distant centuries? —a characteristic scarcity of portable articles of wood ; the isolated box (*arqueta* or *arcón*) which serves the purpose of our clumsier chest of drawers or wardrobe ;[1] carpets and decorated leathers ; the tiny, indispensable table ; the lack of knives and spoons ; ornaments to regale the eye rather than commodities which the hand might seize upon and utilize? Such was, and is, and will continue

[1] Mr Cunninghame Graham, visiting a Caid's house in present-day Morocco, noted, as the only furniture, " leather-covered cushions, the cover cut into intricate geometric patterns ; the room contained a small trunk-shaped box."

20

V

ARMCHAIR

(17th Century. Museum of Salamanca)

FURNITURE

to remain Mohammedan society throughout the world; and these descriptive passages of life in seventeenth-century Morocco might have been penned with equal truth in reference to the Spanish Muslim of a thousand years ago.

The furniture of the Moorish mosques was also of the scantiest. "They are," to quote once more from Lancelot Addison's amusing little brochure, "without the too easy accommodations of seats, pews, or benches. The floor of the Giámma is handsomely matted, and so are the walls about two feet high. If the roof be large and weighty, it is supported with pillars, among which hang the lamps, which are kept burning all the night." At one point of his expedition the reason for such paucity of furniture was vividly expounded to our tourist. A Moor indignantly exclaimed to him that it was "a shame to see women, dogs, and dirty shoes brought into a place sacred to God's worship, and that men . . . . . should have chaires there to sit in with as much lascivious ease as at home."[1]

Nevertheless, a pulpit in the mosque, and a seat of some kind in the palace or the private house, were not to be dispensed with. We learn from

[1] *West Barbary*, p. 150.

ARTS AND CRAFTS OF OLDER SPAIN

Ibn-Khaldoun and many other writers, that the throne of the Mussulman sultans was the *mimbar*, *takcht*, or *cursi*. Each of these objects was a wooden seat. The first of the sultans to use a throne was Moawia, son of Abu-Sofyan. The princes who came after him continued the same usage, but displayed a constantly increasing splendour in the decoration of the throne. This custom spread, in course of time, from east to west throughout almost the whole dominion of the Muslims. The Beni-Nasr princes of Granada are also known to have used a throne, but this is believed to have consisted simply of some cushions piled one upon another. This inference is drawn by Eguilaz Yanguas and other Arabists from the old *Vocabulary* of Fray Pedro de Alcalá, who renders a "throne" or "royal seat" by *martaba*, a word equivalent to "cushion."

Cushions, too, became symbolic, even with the Christian Spaniards, of a seat of honour; both because they lent themselves to rich embroidery or leather-work, and because they raised their occupant above the level of the persons seated positively on the carpet or the floor. In the painting on the ceiling of the Hall of Justice in the Alhambra, ten men are congregated in Moham-

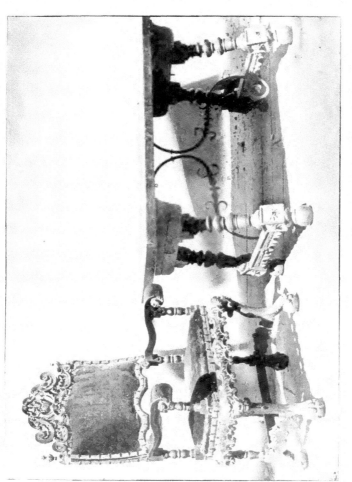

VI

CHAIR AND TABLE

17th Century. Museum at Carlsruhe

medan costume, each of them seated on a cushion.
Some writers, including Argote de Molina, Diego
Hurtado de Mendoza, and Hernando del Pulgar,
believed these figures to be actual portraits of the
sultans; others maintain that they depict the
Mizouar or royal council. In either case, however, the cushion here is clearly an honourable
place. We have, besides, abundant evidence that
the Spanish Christians viewed the cushion with
as marked a liking as their rivals. Alvarez de
Colmenar relates that at the very close of the
seventeenth century the Spanish women sat at
meals in Moorish fashion. " Un père de famille
est assis seul à table, et toutes les femmes, sans
exception, mangent par terre, assises sur un
carreau avec leurs enfans, et leur table dressée
sur un tapis étendu." The same work says elsewhere that "lorsque les dames se rendent visite,
elles ne se donnent ni siège ni fauteuil, mais elles
sont toutes assises par terre, les jambes en croix,
sur des tapis ou des carreaux." [1]

Therefore, until two centuries ago, the women
of Christian Spain were suffered to take their
seat on cushions of brocade or damask. Only
the men made use of stools or chairs, according

[1] *Annales d'Espagne et de Portugal*, vol. iii., pp. 324, 327.

to their rank. To "give a chair" (*dar silla*) to a visitor of the male sex was to pay him a valued courtesy ;[1] and even now the wife of a grandee of Spain goes through the honourable though irksome ceremony, at the palace of Madrid, of "taking the cushion."

Another usage with the Spaniards of the seventeenth and immediately preceding centuries was the "dais of honour" or *estrado de cumplimiento*. This was a platform very slightly raised, and separated by a railing from the rest of the room. The curious manuscript discovered by Gayangos, descriptive of court-life at Valladolid in 1605, contains the following account of one of the occasions when the Queen, following a common custom of a Sunday, dined alone, in sight of all the aristocracy. "The table was laid upon the dais (*estrado alto*), beneath a canopy of brocade that overhung the whole of it. The queen sat at the head of the table, and three ladies, standing, waited on her ; two uncovering the dishes as they came,[2] and the third carving. The

---

[1] "Hónrale el Sr Roberto, alma del Rey, y *le ha dado Silla*, y le tuvo á su lado." Lope de Vega's comedy, *The Key of Honour.*

[2] The covers would be fastened by a lock and key, as a defence, not against poison, but against theft. "A little afterwards Don

24

VII

CHAIRS UPHOLSTERED WITH *GILT LEATHER*

(ABOUT 1650)

FURNITURE

dishes were brought from the dining-room door
by the *meninos*, who handed them to the ladies.
Other ladies of the royal household, wives or
daughters of grandees, stood leaning against the
wall in company with gentlemen who, on such
occasions, sue for leave beforehand to attend on
Lady So and So, or So and So. Commonly
there are two such cavaliers to every dame. If
the queen asks for water, one of these ladies takes
it to her, kneels, makes an obeisance, kisses the
goblet, hands it to her majesty, and retires to her
appointed place. Behind the queen was one of
her chamberlains. Many of the Englishmen
were witnessing the meal. They always put the
English first on such occasions ; and as they are
such hulking fellows (God bless them !) I, who
was at their back, scarce noted anything of what
was passing, and only saw that many plates went
to and fro."

Solid and expensive furniture continued to be

Federico de Cardona, who had gone out to see how matters were
proceeding, returned, bearing a large silver vessel, the cover of
which was secured by a lock and key, as is the custom in Spain."—
Countess d'Aulnoy's *Travels*. As late as the year 1792, Townsend,
in his " Directions to the Itinerant in Spain," recommends (vol. i., p.
2) that the vessel to boil the traveller's meat should be provided with
a cover and a lock.

used in Spain throughout the sixteenth and the seventeenth centuries; the ponderous chest, the ponderous brasier, ponderous stools, ponderous armchairs with massive nails and coverings of velvet or of decorated leather (Plates v., vi., and vii.). Upon the wall, the tapestry of earlier times was often replaced by paintings of a sacred character, or family portraits. The comedy titled *La Garduña de Sevilla*, written about the middle of the seventeenth century by Alonso del Castillo Solorzano, describes the interior of a rich man's dwelling of this period. "Upstairs Rufina noted delicate summer hangings, new chairs of Moscovy cowhide, curiously carved buffets, and ebony and ivory writing-desks: for Marquina, though a skinflint towards others, was generous in the decoration of his own abode. . . . When dinner was over, he took her to a room embellished with fine paintings, and with a bed whose canopy was of some Indian fabric. . . . Paintings by famous masters were plentifully hung about the house, together with fine Italian hangings, various kinds of writing-desks, and costly beds and canopies. When they had visited nearly all the rooms, they opened the door of one which contained a beautiful altar and its oratory. Here were a great array

VIII

26

THE *SALA DE LA BARCA*

(*Before the fire of 1890. Alhambra, Granada*)

of costly and elaborate Roman vessels, agnuses
of silver and of wood, and flowers arranged in
various ways. This chamber, too, was full of
books distributed in gilded cases."

A characteristic piece of Spanish furniture was
at this time the solid-looking cabinet known as the
vargueño, so denominated from the little town
of Vargas, near Toledo, formerly a well-known
centre of their manufacture. These cabinets,
whose origin, according to the Marquis of Monistrol, may be traced to a fifteenth-century form of
huche, or chest provided with drawers for guarding
articles of value, and which opened in the centre,
are commonly made of walnut. The front lets
down upon a massive wooden rest supported by the
legs, and forms a folding writing-table containing at
the back a number of drawers or compartments for
storing documents, or other things of minor bulk.

The woodwork of these cabinets is often without
carving ; but generally in such cases their bare-
ness is relieved by massive and elaborately ornamented iron fastenings and a decorative key.

The Ordinances of Granada tell us that in
1616 the making of defective furniture had grown
to be a scandal in that town. The cause, it
seems, was partly in the wood itself, proceeding

from the Sierra de Segura, Pinar del Duque, and the Sierra de Gor. "Divers of our carpenters and joiners cut their walnut and other woods while yet the moon is crescent, whereby the wood decays and spoils. Others there be that make and sell chairs, desks, beds, and other furniture of green unseasoned wood which warps and loosens, insomuch that within some days the article is worthless. Therefore we order that all walnut wood and other woods for making furniture be only cut at the time of the waning moon, and be not used until they shall have seasoned thoroughly, so as not to warp; and that they be approved by the inspectors of this trade, under a penalty of six thousand *maravedis* for each of the aforesaid Ordinances that be not complied with."

The municipal laws of the same city relative to the "chair-makers who make hip-chairs to sit in, and leather-covered chests," were cried, in 1515 and 1536, "in the street of the chairmakers and carpenters." Fettered by irksome regulations of this kind, we cannot wonder that the arts and crafts of Christian Spain were fated to decline.[1]

[1] The purpose of these Spanish city laws was in its essence unimpeachable; namely, to guard the intensely ignorant Christian

IX

DOOR OF THE HALL OF THE ABENCERRAJES

(Alhambra, Granada)

FURNITURE

Owing to the " false and faulty workmanship " prevailing in Granada, it is provided by these statutes
that the wood employed in making chairs must
be bought by the manufacturers in public auction
only, held "in the little square where dwell the
chairmakers." It must be thoroughly dry and
free from flaws, and of sufficient stoutness to
sustain the decorative marquetry. The chair
which lacks these requisite conditions must be
seized and burnt. The four nails which fasten
the seat of the chair to the legs must traverse the
frame completely and be hammered back upon
the other side, unless the surface of the chair
be inlaid, in which case they need not pass
completely through. The leather for the seats
and backs of chairs must be good in quality and

populace—the same which fugitive Moriscos of the kingdom of
Valencia had readily prevailed upon to barter tons of brass and
pewter trash for sterling gold and silver coin—from being imposed
upon by manufacturers and merchants. But the power of discrimi-
nating between a genuine or well-made object and a piece of
counterfeit or worthless rubbish is, among all peoples, better sought
for and developed by experience than by legislation ; and there was
something noxiously prosaic in a code of city ordinances which
forbade the craftsman to prepare his own design, or choose his
own material, or establish his own prices. How violently, or at
least how primitively, hostile to the sense of art must not have been
these Christian sons of Spain to need—or think they needed—so
impertinent and tyrannous a system of protection !

well prepared and dressed, besides being strongly sewn with flaxen thread. Chairs of all sizes must bear the official city mark, stamped by the authorities at a charge of one *maravedi* for each of the large chairs and a *blanca* for each of the small.

Makers of the leather-covered chests are ordered to use the hides of horses, mares, or mules, and not the hides of oxen, cows, or calves, because, if covered with this latter, "the chests grow moth-eaten and are destroyed much sooner." The craftsman who transgresses this command must lose the faulty piece of furniture, and pay four hundred *maravedis*, while under a further penalty of two hundred *maravedis* the hinges must be fixed inside the chest, and not to its exterior.

I have omitted hitherto all mention of the furnishing of humbler Spanish houses in the olden time. The following passage from the Ordinances of Granada shows us, referring to an inn, an unpretentious lodging of about four hundred years ago :—

"*Item*. If the innkeeper have a parlour or alcove that fastens with a lock, and therein a bed of the better class, with hangings round about it, and a canopy above, and on the bed a

MOORISH DOOR, DETAIL OF CARVING.

(Hall of the Two Sisters, Alhambra, Granada.)

FURNITURE

counterpane, friezed blanket, and pillows ; also a bench with its strip of carpet or striped benchcloth, a table with its service of tablecloths and all that be needful, besides a lamp of brass or ware, all of the best that he is able to provide— for such a bed and room he may demand twelve *maravedis* each day ; whether the room be taken by one guest, or two, or more."[1]

Nor was the Spanish inn more comfortable in the seventeenth or eighteenth centuries than in the sixteenth. "On entre d'ordinaire dans les Hôtelleries par l'écurie, du moins dans de certaines Provinces ; on vous mène dans quelque chambre, où vous trouvez les quatre parois, quelquefois un bois de lit ; pour chandelle on allume un grand nombre de petites bougies, qui font assez de lumière pour voir ce que vous mangez ; et afin que l'odeur and la fumée de tant de bougies n'incommode pas, on vous apporte, si vous le souhaitez, un brasier de noyaux d'olives en charbon. Quand on monte, on trouve au haut de l'escalier, la *Señora de la Casa*, qui a eu le tems de prendre ses beaux habits de dimanche pour vous faire honneur et s'en faire à elle-même." (Alvarez de Colmenar, in 1715.)

[1] *Ordenanza de Mesoneros*, titulo 54.

ARTS AND CRAFTS OF OLDER SPAIN

It is interesting to compare these passages with Lancelot Addison's account of a Morocco inn towards the middle of the seventeenth century ; bearing in mind that *fonda*, the current Spanish term for *hostelry*, is common both to Spain and to Morocco :—

" In later years, every town of traffic hath erected a sort of Inns called *Alfándach*, which affords nothing but House-room for man and beast, the market yielding provision for both. Those that farm these *fandáchs* cannot exact above a Blankil a night both for man and beast, which is in sterling money about two pence. The horses lodging costing equally with his Rider's." [1]

Similarly, the keeper of the older Spanish inn was not allowed by law to traffic in provisions. " Nothing but house-room " was available for way-farers, and the weary visitor, as soon as ever he arrived, must sally forth to do his marketing.

" Quand on arrive aux Hôtelleries, fut il minuit passé, l'on n'y trouve rien de prêt, non pas même un pot sur le feu. L'hôte ne vous donne que le couvert et le lit, pour tout le reste, il le faut en-voyer chercher, si vous ne voulez prendre la peine d'y aller vous-même. On donne l'argent néces-

[1] *West Barbary*, p. 129.

DOOR OF THE *SALON DE EMBAJADORES*

(*Alcazar of Seville*)

saire, et l'on va vous chercher du pain, du vin, de la viande, et généralement tout ce que l'on souhaite, si tant est qu'on le puisse trouver. Il est vrai que cette coutume a son bon côté.

" Le prix de toutes ces choses est règlé, l'on sait ce qu'il faut payer, et un hôte ne peut pas friponner. On vous apprête votre viande, et l'on donne une réale et demie, ou deux réaux pour le *servicio*, comme ils parlent, et autant pour le lit, ce qui revient environ à quinze sous de France. Si l'on se trouve dans quelque grande ville, on aura une nappe grande comme une serviette, et une serviette grande comme un mouchoir de poche ; dans d'autres endroits il faut s'en passer.

" Les lits ne sont pas fort ragoutans ; quelque matelas, ou quelque paillasse, ou tout au plus une couverture de coton ; à la campagne il faut passer la nuit sur le carreau, ou bien sur quelque botte de paille, qu'on doit avoir soin de faire bien secouer, pour en chasser la vermine."

The statements in this passage relative to the lack of food in Spanish hostelries are confirmed, nearly a century later, by Townsend, who records that on reaching a certain village his first proceeding was to turn his steps, not to the *fonda* or *posada* where he would engage his bed, but to the butcher's, wine-seller's, and so forth, "to see what was to be had, as I had travelled all day fasting."

It is beyond the province of this work to dwell upon the foreign taste in furniture which invaded Spain from France upon the advent of the Bourbon dynasty, and so I limit my notice of the eighteenth century to quoting from Laborde the following comprehensive passage :—

"If the Spaniards," this traveller wrote in 1809, "take many precautions against heat, they take scarcely any against cold; it is very uncommon to find doors or windows that shut close, and the rooms are very little and very ill-warmed. The use of chimneys even is very uncommon, and only prevails in the houses of such Spaniards as have travelled. Brasiers of copper or silver are generally employed, which are set in the middle of the apartment, filled with burning charcoal, and round which the family place themselves.

"The beds in Spain are hard. They are only made of mattresses, more or fewer, laid on paillasses which rest upon a boarded bottom ; for neither sacking nor feather beds are known. No

34

DOOR OF THE *SALON DE EMBAJADORES*

Alcázar of Seville

FURNITURE

bolsters are used, but in their place little, short, flat pillows are heaped up, sometimes to the number of six or eight. The sheets are in general short and narrow; and napkins scarcely as big as a small pocket handkerchief.

" The furniture of the houses is usually very simple. The floor is covered with a matting of *esparto* in winter, and of rushes or palm leaves in summer. A matting of the same kind, a painted cloth, or painting in panels, covers the walls from the floor to the height of four or five feet; above, the wall is bare, painted white, and adorned with pictures of saints and a kind of ornamented metal chandeliers; these are covered with a glass, surrounded with a border of gilt ornaments; and a little branch of gilt copper proceeds from them forming zig-zags or festoons, on which the candles are placed; they are called cornucopias; they are from one to three feet in height, and give the apartment the air of a coffee room, or billiard room. Mirrors are placed between the windows, and a lustre of clear glass in imitation of crystal is suspended from the middle of the handsomest saloons. The chairs have straw bottoms; in some provinces, as Murcia, Andalusia, and Valencia, they are of different heights; those on one side of the room being of the common height, and the others one third lower. The latter are intended for the ladies. In some of the principal cities one also sees chairs and sofas of walnut wood, the backs of which are bare, and the seats covered with damask; usually crimson or yellow.

" Luxury begins, however, to show itself in these objects. In the chief cities many hangings are of painted paper or linen; even hangings of brocades, of one and of three colours, and of various other kinds of silk; large and beautiful mirrors, and a number of sofas may be seen. The houses of the grandees in Madrid are magnificently furnished, but usually with more cost than taste. Hangings of silk, velvet, and damask, adorned with rich fringes and gold embroidery, are very common, and the seats are of corresponding magnificence. Many houses in Barcelona, Cadiz, Valencia, and Madrid are decorated with equal study and elegance.

" The custom of painting the walls is of late introducing itself into Spain. They are covered with representations of men and animals, with trees, flowers, landscapes, houses, urns, vases, or history pieces, divided into compartments, adorned

36

XIII

ALCÁZAR OF SEVILLE

(Façade and principal entrance)

FURNITURE

with pillars, pilasters, friezes, cornices, and arabesques; the effect of the whole is often very
agreeable. This kind of decoration was imported
from Italy."[1]

In this account we clearly trace each various
and successive influence that had permeated older
Spain, leaving her, at the close of every period, a
nation that produced illustrious artists, but never
a nation deeply versed in, or devoted to, the arts.
The beds and brasiers of these modern Spaniards
were derived from ancient Rome; their general
dearth of comfortable furniture, together with the
lower, and therefore more humiliating, seats for
women, from the Spanish Moors; the typically
ponderous hangings from mediæval Spain herself; the fresco wall-paintings, such as may still
be seen in many a Spanish country home, from
classic or Renaissance Italy; and the finicking
gilt, rococo cornucopias from France; while the
use of mirrors and of lustres in hideous combination with straw-bottomed chairs, almost reminds us
of the days of Visigothic barbarism.

[1] Vol. v., pp. 301–304.

ARTS AND CRAFTS OF OLDER SPAIN

LEATHER

Guadamacilería, or the art of decorating leather with painting, gilding, and impressions in relief, is commonly believed to have crossed from Africa to Spain at some time in the Middle Ages. According to Duveyrier, the word *guadameci* or *guadamecil* is taken from Ghadames, a town in Barbary where the craft was practised long ago; but Covarrubias gives it an origin directly Spanish, supposing that the title and the craft alike proceeded from a certain town of Andalusia. However this may be, the preparation of these leathers grew to be a most important industry in various parts of Spain, and spread, as time went on, to Italy, France, and other European countries.[1]

In the Peninsula, the principal centres of this work were Cordova, Seville, Lerida, Barcelona, Ciudad Real, and Valladolid. Cordova, however, was so far ahead of all the rest that leathers decorated in this style were known throughout the world as *cueros de Córdoba,* or "Cordova

---

[1] "Spain lays claim to the invention of the art of gilding leather; it is asserted that, after being discovered there, the secret was carried to Naples by Peter Paul Majorano."—Laborde, vol. v., p. 231.

XIV

DOOR OF THE CAPILLA DE LOS VARGAS

(Madrid)

FURNITURE

leathers." Another name for them is said to have been *cordobanes*; but possibly the application of this latter word was less restricted. Bertaut de Rouen wrote in the seventeenth century of Ciudad Real :—"C'est une ville située dans une grande plaine, et dont l'enceinte est assez grande, qui estoit mesme fort peuplée autresfois, mais elle est quasi deserte à present. Il ne luy reste plus rien sinon que c'est là où l'on appreste le mieux les peaux de *Cordouan*, dont on fait les gans d'Espagne. C'est delà aussi d'où elles viennent pour la pluspart à Madrid. J'en achetay quelques-unes."

In 1197 Alfonso the Ninth presented the town of Castro de los Judíos to León Cathedral and its bishop, confirming at the same time the tribute which the Jews who occupied that town were bound to render upon Saint Martin's day in every year, and which consisted of two hundred *sueldos*, a fine skin, and two *guadamecís*. This tribute had existed since the reign of Ferdinand the First : that is, towards the middle of the preceding century.[1]

None of these primitive leathers now exist, and consequently the details of their workmanship

[1] Count of Clonard ; *Memorias para la historia del traje español.*

have perished with them. Ramírez de Arellano mentions two small coffers in the Cluny Museum, which date from about the fourteenth century and are decorated with the forms of animals cut from leather and overlaid on velvet. Other *guadamecís*, though not of the oldest, are in the South Kensington Museum. "The earliest *guadamecileros*," says Ramírez de Arellano, speaking particularly of this art at Cordova, " were accustomed to imitate brocade upon their leathers, employing beaten silver together with the colours red, green, blue, black, white, and carmine, applied in oils, or sometimes (although the law prohibited this) in tempera. Gold was not used till 1529, when Charles the Fifth confirmed the Ordinances of this industry. The leather-workers tanned the hides themselves, stamping the pattern from a wooden mould, and then (if we may call it so) engraving on them. The hides were those of rams. The spaces between the decoration were either coloured red or blue, or simply left the colour of the skin ; or else the pattern would be wrought in colours on the natural hide. Gold, which at a later epoch almost totally replaces silver, was introduced between 1529 and 1543, and was

40

XV

MUDEJAR DOOR

(Palacio de las Dueñas, Seville)

FURNITURE

applied as follows. The artists smeared with oil the parts they wished to figure in raised or sunk relief, and laid the beaten gold upon the oil. They then applied a heated iron or copper mould ; the pattern in relief was stamped ; and the gold, superfluous shreds of which were wiped away with lint, adhered upon the leather. The irons required to be moderately hot, because if overheated they would burn the hide, or, if not hot enough, the fixing of the gold would not be permanent."

The importance of this industry in Spain may be judged of from the fact that towards the close of the Middle Ages the *guadamacileros* of Seville occupied nearly the whole of an important street— the Calle Placentines. Similarly, at Cordova they filled the quarter of the city known as the Ajerquía. "So many *guadamecíes* are made here," wrote Ambrosio de Morales, "that in this craft no other capital can compare with her ; and in such quantities that they supply all Europe and the Indies. This industry enriches Cordova and also beautifies her ; for since the gilded, wrought, and painted leathers are fixed upon large boards and placed in the sun in order to be dried, by reason of their splendour and variety they make her principal streets right fair to look upon."

ARTS AND CRAFTS OF OLDER SPAIN

We owe to Rafael Ramírez de Arellano most valuable and recent information respecting this ancient Spanish-Moorish craft.[1] He has discovered the names of nearly forty *guadamacileros* who lived and worked at Cordova, principally in the sixteenth century. It is not worth while to repeat these names alone, but one or two particulars connected with a few of them are interesting. In 1557 four of these artificers, named Benito Ruiz, Diego de San Llorente, Diego de Ayora, and Anton de Valdelomar, signed a contract to prepare the cut and painted *guadamaciles* for decorating a palace at Rome. This contract, which is most precise and technical, is published in No. 101 of the *Boletín de la Sociedad Española de Excursiones*. The only further notice which Señor Ramírez de Arellano has discovered relating to any of these four craftsmen, tells us that nine years after the signing of the document just mentioned, Diego de Ayora leased some houses in the Calle de la Feria for a yearly rental of twenty-two ducats and three pairs of live hens.

Another interesting contract is dated April 17th, 1587. By it the *guadamacilero* Andrés

[1] *Boletín de la Sociedad Española de Excursiones*, Nos. 101, 102 ; Art. *Guadamacies.*

XVI

CELOSÍA.
(Alhambra, Granada)

FURNITURE

Lopez de Valdelomar agreed, in company with Hernando del Olmo of Marchena, and with Francisco de Gaviria and Francisco Delgado, painters, of Cordova, to make a number of pieces of *guadameci* for the Duke of Arcos. The work was to be terminated by July of the same year. Valdelomar was to receive from the duke's agent three *reales* for each piece, and the painters two *reales* and a half; this money to be paid them by instalments as the work proceeded.

On August 26th, 1567, before the mayor of Cordova and the two inspectors of this trade, Pedro de Blancas was officially examined and approved in "cutting, working, and completing a *guadameci* of red damask with gold and silver borders on a green field, and a cushion with green and crimson decoration and faced with silver brocade."

The Ordinances of Cordova also tell us much about this industry. The oldest of these city laws which deal with it are dated 1529. Those of 1543 were ratified by a Crown pragmatic early in the seventeenth century, and at this later date we learn that the craft had much declined, the leather being by now "of wretched quality, the colouring imperfect, and the pieces undersized." The Ordinances published in the sixteenth century

43

provide that every applicant for official licence to pursue this craft and open business as a *guadama-cilero*, must prove himself, in presence of the examiners, able to mix his colours and design with them, and to make a canopy together with its fringe, as well as "a cushion of any size or style that were demanded of him ; nor shall he explain merely by word of mouth the making of the same, but make it with his very hands in whatsoever house or place shall be appointed by the mayor and the overseers of the craft aforesaid."

It was also provided by these Ordinances that the pieces of leather were to be dyed, not with Brazil-wood, but with madder, and that their size, whether the hide were silvered, gilt, or painted, was to be strictly uniform, namely, "the size of the primitive mould," or "three-quarters of a yard in length by two-thirds of a yard, all but one inch, in width." The standard measures, made of iron and stamped with the city seal, were guarded under lock and key ; and the Ordinances of 1567 establish the penalty of death for every *guadamacilero* who shall seek, in silvering his wares, to palm off tin for silver.

These leathers served a great variety of purposes, public or private, sacred or profane.

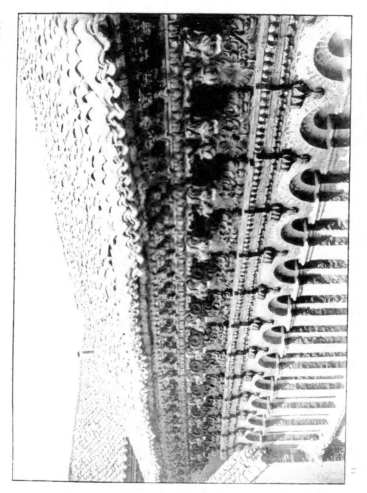

XVII

CARVED ALTAR

FURNITURE

They were used upon the walls and floors of palaces and castles, as table-covers, counterpanes, bed-hangings, cushions, curtains for doors, linings for travelling-litters, coverings of chests and boxes,[1] and seats and backs of chairs and benches (Plate vii.). In churches and cathedrals, especially throughout the sixteenth century, we find them used as tapestry and carpets,[2] altar-fronts (such as one which is preserved in the chapel of San Isidro in Palencia cathedral), or crowns for images of the Virgin.[3] As time advanced, gold and a coat or so of colour was

---

[1] The *Poem of the Cid* tells us of the two chests, covered with red *guadameci*, which the hero filled with sand to cheat the Jewish money-lenders :—

> " *Con vuestro consejo bastir quiero dos archas.*
> *Incamosla d'arena, cá bien serán pesadas.*
> *Cubiertas de guadameci é bien enclavadas ;*
> *Los guadamecis bermeios é los clavos bien dorados.*"

Nevertheless, the "coffer of the Cid" at Burgos (see p. 12) does not appear to have been thus fitted.

[2] The same usage obtained in Morocco. Lancelot Addison wrote in 1669 that on the first day of their " Little Feast" the Moors across the Strait "spread the floor of their Giammas with coloured leather."—*West Barbary*, p. 213.

[3] An inventory of effects belonging to the Hospital of San José at Jerez de la Frontera mentions, in 1589, "clothes and trimmings for the image of Our Lady. A crown of gilded *guadameci.*"—Gestoso, *Diccionario de Artifices Sevillanos*, vol. i., p. xxii, *note*.

succeeded by elaborate painting. Thus painted, they were often cut into the forms of columns, pilasters, or friezes in the Plateresco or Renaissance style,[1] until the growing popularity of wall-pictures, together with the importation of French fashions at the death of Charles the Second, crippled and ultimately killed the decorative leather industry of Spain.

CARPENTRY AND WOOD-CARVING

The artistic carpentry of older Spain produced as its most typical and striking monuments, three

[1] A hall, says Ramírez de Arellano, would often be embellished by surrounding it with arches wrought of leather in relief and superposed on leather. As a rule the arches were gilt and silvered, and rested upon pilasters or columns. When pilasters were used, their centres would be ornamented with Italian devices such as flowers, trophies, imitated cameos, and foliage. Landscapes with a far horizon and no figures, known as *boscaje* or *pintura verde* were painted on the space between the arches, so that the general effect was that of a pavilion with arches on all sides, displaying everywhere a wide expanse of fertile country. The arches rested on a broad bordering of *guadamecíes*, and running round the lower part was a *zócalo* or socle, commonly made of tiling.

Such is the kind of decoration which was most in vogue in Spain throughout the latter half of the sixteenth century ; that which was exported to Rome ; and that which was commissioned by the Duke of Arcos.

XVIII

CARVED ZAPATAS

(Casa de Salinas, Salamanca)

FURNITURE

groups of objects which may be included generally under Furniture. These are the *celosía* or window-lattice, the door of *lazo*-work, and the *artesonado*-ceiling which adorns a hall or chamber, corridor or staircase.

These happy and effective styles of decoration came originally from the East. Their passage may be traced along the coast of Africa from Egypt into Spain; and they flourished in Spain for the same reason which had caused them to flourish at Cairo. "When we remember," says Professor Lane-Poole, "how little wood grows in Egypt, the extensive use made of this material in the mosques and houses of Cairo appears very remarkable. In mosques, the ceilings, some of the windows, the pulpit, lectern or Koran desk, tribune, tomb-casing, doors, and cupboards, are of wood, and often there are carved wooden inscriptions and stalactites of the same material leading up to the circle of the dome. In the older houses, ceilings, doors, cupboards, and furniture are made of wood, and carved lattice windows, or meshrebiyas, abound. In a cold climate, such employment of the most easily worked of substances is natural enough; but in Egypt, apart from the scarcity of the material, and the necessity of importing it, the heat offers serious obstacles to its use. A plain board of wood properly seasoned may keep its shape well enough in England, but when exposed to the sun of Cairo it will speedily lose its accurate proportions; and when employed in combination with other pieces, to form windows or doors, boxes or pulpits, its joints will open, its carvings split, and the whole work will become unsightly and unstable. The leading characteristic of Cairo wood-work is its subdivision into numerous panels; and this principle is obviously the result of climatic considerations, rather than any doctrine of art. The only mode of combating the shrinking and warping effects of the sun was found in a skilful division of the surfaces into panels small enough, and sufficiently easy in their setting, to permit of slight shrinking without injury to the general outline. The little panels of a Cairo door or pulpit may expand without encountering enough resistance to cause any cracking or splitting in the surrounding portions, and the Egyptian workmen soon learned to accommodate themselves to the conditions of their art in a hot climate."[1]

These valuable and interesting observations

[1] *The Art of the Saracens in Egypt*, pp. 124, 125.

XIX

CARVED ZAPATAS

(Museum of Zaragoza)

FURNITURE

apply with equal justice to the decorative woodwork of the Spanish Muslims. A further point
of interest lies in the fact that window-grilles and
ceilings of the kind referred to, grew to be extremely fashionable through the whole Peninsula.
Carried by Moorish or Mudejar craftsmen far
beyond the frontiers of the Mussulman sultans of
this European land, we find to-day surviving
specimens in every part of Spain—most of them,
it is true, in sultry Andalus; but many also in the
old seigniorial mansions of Castile, or even in
the cold and humid towns and cities of Cantabria.

The man who did this kind of work was not a
common carpenter. Such work was largely practical and prosaic, but also it was largely decorative
and poetical. Probably, both in his own and in
his customer's regard, the decorative quality was
set before the practical. Therefore, beyond the
dry, comparatively facile details of technique, this
workman studied, with an artist's reverence and
zeal, the inner, subtler, sweeter mysteries of line
and form; harmonies of curve and angle; patterns,
now geometrical, now floral, now these two combined with magic ingenuity; steeping himself in
the æsthetic sense; making, indeed, his work the
literal fact or fitting of prosaic application that

was indispensable ; but also, and as if upon some loftier initiative of his own, a miracle of art for people of a later day to come and stand before and wonder at.

Indeed, whether because Our Lord had practised it, or from some other motive, carpentry was always well esteemed among the Spaniards. The Ordinances of Seville eulogize it, in conjunction with its sister-work of masonry and building, as " a noble art and self-contained, that increaseth the nobleness of the King and of his kingdom, that pacifieth the people, and spreadeth love among mankind, conducing to much good." [1] The same Ordinances divide these honourable craftsmen into half a dozen classes and sub-classes ; carvers or *entalladores*, carpenters who kept a shop (*carpinteros de tienda*), *carpinteros de lo prieto*, and *carpinteros de lo blanco*. The latter are the class we are considering here, and these, in turn, were subdivided into *lazeros* or makers of *lazo*-work, *non-lazeros* or those who did not make it, and *jumetricos* or *geómetricos*. The statutory

[1] " *Es noble arte, complida en sí; è acrescienta la nobleza del rey y del reyno, si en ella pararen mientes, como deuen; è pone paz en el pueblo y amor entre los omes, onde es carrera para muchos bienes.*"—*Ordenanzas de Sevilla*, Part I, p. 141.

XX

50

ALERO AND CORNICE OF CARVED WOOD

(Cuarto de Comares, Alhambra, Granada)

examination was severe in all these branches. Thus, the *lazero*-carpenters of Seville were required to make a chamber of octagonal *lazo*-work, including its pendentives at the corners; while the wood-carvers of the same city were required to be experienced draughtsmen and to make and carve "artistic altar-screens with decorated columns, pedestals for images, and tabernacles (*i.e.* the part of an altar where the cibory and the Host are kept), as well as tombs and chambranles with their covering, tabernacles of the utmost art (*de grande arte*), and rich choir-stalls."

Nor was the making of artistic ceilings, doors, and window-gratings carried out exclusively by men of Moorish blood. Tutored by these, the Christians practised it with great success. Prominent among these last we find, early in the seventeenth century, the name of Diego Lopez de Arenas, a Christian-Spaniard and a native of Marchena, who held the licensed title of master-carpenter and lived for many years at Seville.[1] In a lucky moment it occurred to Lopez de Arenas to write and publish for the benefit of his

[1] Gestoso finds no record of him in the city archives; but from a rough portrait of Arenas prefixed to his treatise, we judge that he was born about the year 1580.

fellow-craftsmen a book upon this decorative oriental woodwork that had passed into the Spanish national life. This book, *Carpintería de lo Blanco*,[1] appeared at Seville in 1633, and fresh editions were printed at the same city in 1727, and at Madrid in 1867. As in the Ordinances of Granada, Seville, and Toledo, Arabic terms, too copious and too complicated for elucidation here, are constantly repeated in this book.[2] Much of the general information which we gather from it is, however, of great interest. Thus, we are told that with the Spanish artists, as in Egypt, the wood most often used, no doubt as being the cheapest, was pitch pine, parcelled and put together in the most elaborate decorative schemes. Such was the characteristic *alfarge*[3] ceiling of the Moorish, Morisco, and Spanish-Christian *carpintero de lo blanco*. Its many fragments were secured upon the frame by long,

---

[1] Arenas himself defines a *carpintero de lo blanco* as "he who prepares and works upon the wood employed in building ; also, he who fashions tables, benches, etc., in his workshop."

[2] "His language abounds in Arabic words and phrases of uncertain origin, whose meaning (since he wrote for men familiar with this work) he makes no effort to explain."—Editor's introduction to the third edition of *Carpintería de lo Blanco*.

[3] Arabic *al-farx*, a carpet, piece of tapestry, or anything that covers and adorns.

XXI

" ELIJAH SLEEPING "

(Statue in wood, by Alonso Cano)

FURNITURE

small-headed nails, or by these nails combined with glue. If we observe the ceilings from close by, as when, for instance, they are taken down to be restored, the workmanship appears to be coarse, inaccurate, and hasty; the myriad pieces to be clumsily and loosely joined; the nails to be driven in without method, or even awry. Nevertheless, this false effect betrays the calculating genius of the craftsman. He planned his work for contemplation by a certain light and at a certain elevation; and therefore, as the ceiling is removed again to its appointed distance, it seems to re-create itself in proud defiance of an error of our own, and grows at once to its habitual delicacy, harmony, and richness.

I have said that the decoration of these ceilings is sometimes floral, sometimes geometrical, sometimes a combination of the two.[1] Sometimes the wood is plain, or sometimes silvered, gilt, or painted. Sometimes it is employed alone, or sometimes variegated and inlaid with plaster points and patches. By far the commonest

[1] This mingled decoration is extremely common; and may be studied in our country, in the carved panels at South Kensington which are believed to proceed from the pulpit of the mosque of Kusun; or in the thirteenth-century panels of the tomb of Es-salih Ayyub.

motive is the *lazo*—an ornamental scheme composed of infinite strips that turn, and twist, and intersect, describing in their mazy passage many polygons. One of these polygons determines, in a way, the scheme of the entire ceiling, which is denominated as consisting of "a *lazo* of eight," "of ten," "of twelve," etc., from this particular. The most attractive and most frequent is the scheme "of eight." Among the decorative details used to brighten and enhance the *lazo* proper are *mocarabes* or wooden lacery for relieving cubes and joists or surfaces, and *rácimos* or "clusters"; that is, hollow or solid wooden cones or prisms, disposed along the side and centre panels of the ceiling like (in Arenas' ingenious phrase) the buttons on a jacket, and contributing to the massive aspect of the whole. These clusters, too, were sometimes in the stalactite and sometimes in a simpler form, and show, both in the quantity and richness of their ornament, a limitless diversity.

Magnificent Spanish-Moorish, Spanish, and Mudejar ceilings still exist in Spain. Such are the marvellous domed ceiling in the Hall of Comares (or of Ambassadors) in the Alhambra, those of the Castle of the Aljafería at Zara-

XXII

SAINT BRUNO

(By Alonso Cano, Cartuja of Granada)

FURNITURE

goza and of the archbishop's palace at Alcalá de
Henares, the Arab *alfarge* ceilings in the
churches of San Francisco and Santiago of
Guadix, that of the Hall of Cortes in the Audiencia
of Valencia, that of the Sala Capitular of Toledo
Cathedral, that of the Chapel of the Holy Spirit
of the Cathedral of Cuenca (considered by many
to be the finest *artesonado* ceiling in all Spain),
or those of the churches of Jesus Crucificado,
El Carmen, and San Pablo at Cordova. The
ceiling of the Sala de la Barca, in the Moorish
palace of the Alhambra, was almost totally destroyed by fire in 1890, but a good photograph
had previously been taken, and I reproduce it
here (Plate viii.). One of the later *artesonado*
ceilings is at Cordova, in the parish church
of Santiago. Covered with a *bóveda* or vault
of cane, it is in excellent preservation, and was
made in 1635 by the master-carpenter Alonso
Muñoz de los Ríos, who received for his labour
fourteen thousand *reales*.[1] The *artesonado* ceilings

[1] Cordova was a famous centre of this craft for many centuries.
Ramírez de Arellano has found and published a notice relative to
Lope de Liaño and García Alonso, two artificers of this city who
signed, on January 7th, 1572, a contract with the prior of the monastery of the Holy Martyrs to build a ceiling for one of the chapels
of the same. The document, which is quoted *in extenso* in the

which Diego Lopez de Arenas tells us in his treatise that he made for the church, the choir, and the *sobreescalera* of the monastery of Santa Paula at Seville, as well as a ceiling which he made for the church of Mairena, are all extant to-day. Other remarkable examples of this craft are the ceilings of the rooms constructed to the order of, and which were actually occupied by, Charles the Fifth, within the precincts of the old Alhambra. Upon these half-Italian, half-Morisco ceilings and their frieze we read the words, "*Plus Oultre*"; and the inscription, "*Imperator Cæsar Karolus V. Hispaniarum rex semper augustus pius fœlix invictissimus.*" In one of the same apartments, known as the "chamber of the fruits," the ceiling has octagonal *artesones* of superb effect, though even richer is that of what is called the Second Sala de las Frutas, conspicuously influenced by Italian art, and believed by Gómez

Boletín de la Sociedad Española de Excursiones for November, 1900, abounds in technical expressions, many of them partly or entirely Moorish.

The same writer publishes the names (hitherto completely unrecorded) of thirteen other artist-carpenters who worked at Cordova in the latter half of the sixteenth century and early in the seventeenth. The craft, in fact, died hard, and ceilings of this kind, replete with Moorish detail, were made in certain parts of Southern Spain until the closing moments of the eighteenth century.

XXIII

SAINT JOHN THE BAPTIST

(San Juan de Dios, Granada)

FURNITURE

Moreno to have been designed by Pedro Machuca
and executed by Juan de Plasencia.

Marvellous in conjunction with the thousand
lighted lamps which served to manifest its beauties,
must have been the primitive ceiling (*as-sicafes*)
of the mosque of Cordova, of which an Arab poet
sang; "Look at the gold on it, like the kindled
flame, or like the lightning-stroke that darts
across the heavens."[1] Our notices of this ceiling,
barbarously hacked to pieces by Christian architects, are neither numerous nor clear. We are
told, however, that it was nearly finished in the
reign of Abd-er-Rhaman the First, and terminated
altogether by his son Hixem. New ceilings were
added on the enlarging of the mosque by Abd-er-
Rhaman the Second, while fresh additions were
made by Al-Hakem the Second and Al-Manzor.
Ambrosio de Morales gives a quaint description
of the earliest, or an early, ceiling of this temple.
"The roof of the whole church, made of wood
painted and adorned in divers ways, is of incredible
richness, as will be seen from what I am about to

---

[1] That the Moors were proud of their mastery in woodwork is
proved by an inscription in the Torre de la Cautiva at Granada,
saying; "In the plaster and the tiles is work of extreme beauty,
but the woodwork of the roof has vanquished them in elegance."

57

say.   It is of larch throughout, odorous, resembling pine, which is not found in any part but Barbary,[1] whence it is brought by sea.   And every time that a part of this temple was thrown down for new constructions to be added, the wood removed was sold for many thousand ducats for making guitars and other delicate objects.   The ceiling was built across the church upon the nineteen naves thereof, and over it, covered likewise with wood, the roofs, nineteen in number also, each with its ridge atop, drooping to one and other side."[2]

Three pieces made of common pine, and which are thought to have belonged to the original ceiling of this mosque or to an early replica, are now in the National Museum at Madrid, but the carving of these fragments is so simple that in the opinion of Rodrigo Amador de los Ríos the decoration of the wood itself was purposely subordinated in this instance to the richness and variety of the painting.

Three types of decorative doors were made in

[1] Morales was probably mistaken. "On entering Aragon one sees whole forests of ' Spanish Cedar' or *alerce*, some of the trees so thick that they measure four feet in diameter."—Bowles' *Natural History of Spain*, p. 102.

[2] *Antigüedades de las ciudades de España* (A.D. 1575), p. 123.

XXIV

CHOIR-STALLS

(Santo Tomás, Ávila)

FURNITURE

older Spain. In the earliest and simplest (*lacería en talla*), the *lacería* or *lazo*-work is carved directly on and from the solid plank which forms the body of the door. In the second type, the carver's art is delicately blended with the joiner's—*lazo*-work with *ensamblaje*. In the third type the *lazo*-work is *sobrepuesta*—that is, attached to, not elaborated from, the planking.[1]

As in the case of ceilings, many and excellent examples of these doors exist to-day in Spain. Among the most remarkable are several in the Moorish palace of the Alhambra, such as the two (dating from the end of the fourteenth century or early in the fifteenth) belonging, respectively, to the famous Hall of the Abencerrajes (Pl. ix.), and to the Hall of the Two Sisters (Pl. x.). Apparently it was the former of these doors which Bertaut de Rouen wrote of in the seventeenth century as " une porte aussi grande et aussi épaisse comme celles de nos plus grandes églises. Elle s'ouvre

---

[1] José Amador de los Ríos mentions, as a good example of the first of these types, a thirteenth-century door of the *claustrilla* in the monastery of Las Huelgas at Burgos. Other doors in the same monastery are illustrative of the second type ; while all three types are represented by the doors, described herewith, which close the principal entrance to the misnamed Hall of Ambassadors in the Alcázar of Seville.

des deux costez, et est toute de pieces rapportées, et d'un bois de differentes couleurs, comme les beaux cabinets et les belles tables qui coustent si cher." [1]

An early Mudejar door proceeding from the church of San Pedro at Daroca in Aragon is now in the National Museum. This door, which is of larch, and measures nearly fourteen feet in height by nine in breadth, is of a simple design and represents a horse-shoe door described within the door itself. It was originally painted vermilion, with other decorative painting of a simple character in black, white, and red, and is fortified with massive iron braces. It is believed to date from earlier than the fourteenth century.

The mighty doors of the "Hall of Ambassadors," in the mediæval royal residence of Seville (Plates xi. and xii.), are quite the finest to be seen in Spain. Although a widespread superstition assigns their manufacture to a period close upon the Moorish conquest, it has been proved conclusively that they were made by Mudejar craftsmen of Toledo at the time when the whole Alcázar was erected more or less upon the ruins of the old, by Pedro the First of Castile, denominated, according to

[1] *Journal du Voyage en Espagne*, p. 85.

XXV

CARVED CHOIR-STALL.

(*Toledo Cathedral*)

the prejudice with which we view his character, "the Cruel," or "the Just." [1]

These doors, which under a pretence of restoration have been mutilated more than once, are made of larch, and measure sixteen feet in height by thirteen feet (including both the leaves) in width. The upper part of either leaf consists of geometrical and floral ornament in exquisitely tasteful combination, executed in the scheme known technically, from the angles at the central polygon, as *lazo de á doce*—"*lazo*-work of twelve." The

---

[1] The following words record the date of the construction of this place and its doors, and may be read (Plate xiii.) upon the scroll of tiles or *alizares* crowning the principal façade :—

✠ EL : MUY : ALTO : ET : MUY : NOBLE : ET : MUY : PODEROSO : ET : MUY : CONQUERIDOR : DON : PEDRO : POR : LA : GRACIA : DE : DIOS : REY : DE : CASTIELLA : ET : DE : LEON : MANDÓ : FACER : ESTOS : ALCÁZARES : ET : ESTOS : PALACIOS : ET : ESTAS : PORTADAS : QUE : FUÉ : FECHO : EN : LA : ERA : DE : MILL : ET : QUATROÇIENTOS : Y : DOS :

The observant Swinburne was not misled, like many travellers of to-day, into believing the Alcázar to be of purely Moorish origin. "Having read that the Moors built one part of this palace, I concluded I was admiring something as old as the Mahometan kings of Seville ; but upon closer examination was not a little surprised to find *lions, castles,* and other armorial ensigns of Castille and Leon, interwoven with Arabesque foliages ; and still more so, to see in large Gothic characters, an inscription informing me that these edifices were built in the fourteenth century, by the most mighty king of Castille and Leon, Don Pedro."

decoration of the lower part is more minute, and in the scheme of *lazo de á diez*—"*lazo*-work of ten." Inscriptions in Arabic and Latin, many of which are quoted from the Psalms, are distributed on both sides of the woodwork, and confirm our other evidence that the doors were made during the reign and in obedience to the orders, of Don Pedro.

The Plateresco sixteenth-century doors of the Capilla de los Vargas at Madrid (Plate xiv.) are attributed by Cean Bermudez and by Ponz to an artist named Giralte, who carved them in walnut with various military and other scenes from Scripture, alternating with shields and floral ornament ; the whole surrounded by an exquisitely delicate and tasteful border. Lampérez remarks that the errors of perspective recall the similar productions of Ghiberti.

The *celosía* or decorative wooden window-grating, imported by the Mussulman conqueror from Egypt and the East, extended to all parts of Christian Spain, and was particularly used in convents. These gratings, identical in form and workmanship with those of Cairo,[1] were attached

[1] " The windows, which are chiefly composed of curious wooden lattice-work, serving to screen the inhabitants from the view of persons without, as also to admit both light and air, commonly pro-

CHOIR STALLS

(Burgos Cathedral)

to projecting windows, so that the women of a household could look into the street without themselves being seen, a custom which the Spanish woman still recalls to us by peering, for hours at a time, between the lowered *persiana* of her balcony.[1] By the seventeenth century, which may truthfully be called the age of Spanish jealousy, and when the " Othello-like revenge of the Moor" had eaten into the very entrails of society, the *celosía* had become as indispensable to houses as the door or window. " La," wrote Bertaut de Rouen of a residence on the outskirts of Madrid, and obviously alluding to these gratings, "il y avoit bien des Dames dans l'appartement d'enhaut qui y demeurerent cachées, se contentant de nous voir promener dans le jardin par les fenêtres."

We know from the stone coat of arms which is carved above the doorway of the " House of Castril at Granada" that in the olden time the

ject outwards, and are furnished with mattresses and cushions."— Lane's *Arabian Nights*, vol. i., p. 192.

[1] It is strange that Ford should have confounded the *reja* with the *celosía* (*Handbook*, vol. i., p. 153). However, he opportunely quotes the Spanish proverb, *Muger ventanera tuercela el cuello si la quieres buena* (" The remedy for a woman who is always thrusting her head from the casement is to twist her neck ").

balconies of the Hall of Comares in the Alhambra were fitted with projecting wooden *celosías* ; and Contreras says that in the Torre de los Puñales of the same palace there used to be "a kind of wooden *mirador* or *menacir*, covered with *celosías* like those of Cairo, and many of which were still to be seen in Granada early in the nineteenth century."

I am not aware of any Moorish *celosía* remaining to this day outside a Spanish building. In such exposed positions weather and the natural delicacy of the woodwork seem to have destroyed them all. As an interior ornament, a single one (Pl. xvi.) exists in the Alhambra. Nevertheless, I hesitate to call this *celosía* purely Moorish. Perhaps it is the work of a Morisco, or even of a Christian-Spaniard, for we know that decorative wooden fittings for the Alhambra were made in the sixteenth century by Antonio Navarro and other craftsmen. The grating, which is well preserved, covers a window over the archway leading from the Hall of the Two Sisters into the Sala de los Ajimeces and the Mirador de Daraxa, and consists of minute prisms and turned pieces in the typical Egyptian style.

Other fittings for a building, wrought in wood

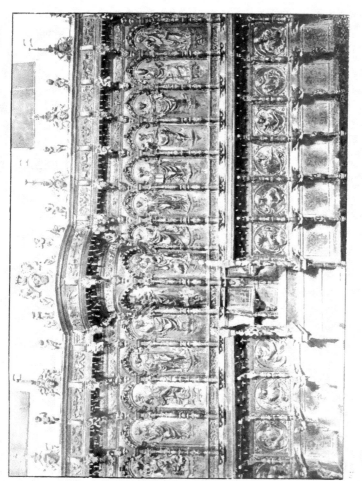

XXVII

CHOIR STALLS

(San Marco, Lucca)

FURNITURE

by Moorish artists and by these communicated
to the Christian-Spaniards, were balustrades and
cornices, *aleros* (decorative bands beneath the
eaves of a roof, Plate xvii.) and *zapatas* (gargoyle-
looking figures, often in human form, used to
support a roof or gallery). In the so-called "Patio
de las Asas" of the convent of Santa Catalina de
Zafra, at Granada, exists an interesting Moorish
balustrade [1] that seems almost untouched by time.
I reproduce an outline of it as the tailpiece to the
present chapter, and am glad to append the little
sketch in question, copied from a photograph I
took upon the spot three years ago, because it
is almost impossible to obtain admission to this
convent. Beautiful or uncouth and quaint *zapatas*
may be seen in the Casa de los Tiros at Granada,
and in many other places (Plates xviii. and xix.).
Much of the Moorish woodwork of the palace of
the Alhambra was destroyed by the fire of 1590,
but there yet remain the ample cornice and carved

---

[1] Almagro Cardenas calls it "part of a *celosía*" (*Museo Granadino*,
p. 79) ; but as it can never have been a window-grating, this term is
incorrect. Gómez Moreno calls it, not too lucidly, "a wooden balustrade forming squares and rectangular figures in the manner of a
celosía" (*Guía de Granada*, p. 421). Valladar (*Guía de Granada*,
edition of 1906, p. 117) calls it simply a balustrade, and this, it
seems to me, is the only term which truthfully describes the object.

alero of the façade of the Cuarto de Comares
(Plate xx.), which is often called in error the
Court of the Mezquita. This *alero* bears the
following inscription, allusive to the Sultan Mohammed the Fifth :—" I am the place where the
crown is guarded, and on my doors being opened
the regions of the west believe the east to be contained within me. Algami Billah charged me to
keep guard upon the doorway."

Other remarkable *aleros* are in the Generalife
and in the Court of Lions of the Alhambra, while,
also in this last-named mansion, genuine Moorish
woodwork of elaborately inlaid ebony and larch
is in two niches near the entrance to the Sala de
Embajadores.

SACRED STATUARY, *SILLERÍAS* OR CHOIR-STALLS, AND *RETABLOS*

The genius of the wood-carvers of older Spain
is manifested chiefly in three groups of objects—
sacred statuary, choir-stalls, and *retablos*. Among
this people, and probably by reason of its cheap-
ness, plain, or gilt, or polychrome painted wood has
always been a favourite material for the statues
of their temples, whether such statues were em-

XXVIII

DETAIL OF CHOIR-STALLS

(León Cathedral)

FURNITURE

ployed alone, or as an accessory to a larger article
of sacred furniture, such as a pulpit, or a *sillería*,
or an altar-screen. So powerful, in fact, has been
the vogue of this material here,[1] that even to-day
the Spanish people, making, in Symonds' happy
phrase, "representation an object in itself, inde-
pendently of its spiritual significance," attempt to
elevate the most remarkable of their wooden,

[1] My readers are no doubt aware that every Spanish hamlet has
its wooden image of the Virgin, badly executed as a rule, and
rendered doubly hideous by a gaudy gown. Most of these local
images are believed to hold the power of working miracles, or at
least to have been fashioned and conducted to their present shrine
by supernatural agency—on which account the populace and their
pastors call these latter *imagenes aparecidas*, as distinct from *manufactured* images. Such are the Virgins of Montserrat, Granada,
and numerous other cities, towns, or villages of this illiterate and
ill-starred Peninsula. The curious may refer for every kind of
detail to Villafañe's *Compendious History of the Wonder-working
Images of Spain*, which numbered in this author's day (his book
was published in 1740) one hundred and eighty-nine. But the most
extraordinary miracle of all was that which is recalled, with pious
gravity, by Bertaut de Rouen. Speaking of the gilt-wood image of
Nuestra Señora del Pilar at Zaragoza, he says :—" On y void quantité de lampes d'argent et on m'en raconta un miracle qu'il me
fut impossible de ne pas croire. C'est d'un pauvre homme qui
ayant eu la jambe coupée pour une blessure, et s'estant bien recom-
mandé à *Nostra Señora del Pilar*, il se trouva un jour avec sa mesme
jambe qu'il avoit déja fait enterrer. Y'ay sceu l'histoire du chirurgien
mesme qui coupa cette jambe et de quantité de témoins de veuë.
Il n'y a que quinze ans que cela est arrivé, mais l'homme est mort
depuis peu."—*Journal du Voyage en Espagne*, p. 203.

and by preference their coloured wooden, statuary (typically defended by Pacheco's indigested tome), to rank beside the noblest and the purest monuments of bronze and marble ; denoting, by this reckless and uneducated partiality, a positively national misconception of the true domain of art.

It is outside the scope of such a work as this to deal at any length with Spanish figure-sculpture. However, it is only fair to recognize that Spain produced a couple of score or so of admirable carvers of wood-statuary. Among the greatest of these craftsmen or *imagineros* were Becerra, Berruguete, Juan de Juni, author of the *Mater Dolorosa* ("Our Lady of the Knives"), of Valladolid ; Gregorio Hernández the Galician, author of "Simon the Cyrenian," "Santa Veronica," and "the Baptism of our Lord" ; Martínez Montañes, author of "San Jerónimo" and of the "Cristo del Gran Poder" ;[1] Solis, Gaspar de Ribas, Juan Gómez, author of the "Jesus" of Puerto de Santa Maria ; Pedro Roldan, with whom, according to Tubino, "the

[1] It is due to Martínez Montañes to mention that in many of his contracts he stipulated that the painters of his statuary should be chosen by himself, "so as not to corrupt the outline and the sentiment of the figures."

68

XXIX

CHOIR-STALLS

(*Plasencia Cathedral*)

FURNITURE

art of Seville closed its eyes"; and Alonso Cano, master of Pedro and Alonso de Mena, Ruiz del Peral, José de Mora, and Diego de Mora, and who carved the exquisite "Elijah Sleeping" (Pl. xxi.) now at Toledo, and also (as it is believed) the famous statuette (Frontispiece to the present volume) of Saint Francis of Assisi.

The earliest centre of this branch of wood-carving was Valladolid, where lived and laboured Juni and Hernández. Nevertheless, although so popular in every part of Spain, it had a short-lived prime, originating in the two Castiles towards the reign of Philip the Second, declining steadily (with Seville for its centre now) all through the seventeenth century, and flickering out, despite the perseverance and the genius of the Murcian Susillo, in the century succeeding.

In decorative *sillerías* or sets of choir-stalls, Spain has produced examples worthy to be set beside the masterpiece of Vitry in the abbey of Sainte-Claude, the best productions of Dürer and his followers in Germany, or those of Donatello, Brunelleschi, Valdambrino, Vechietta, and Verrochio in Italy. Nevertheless, her most distinguished *sillería*-makers were at almost every moment inspired and directed by the foreigner.

ARTS AND CRAFTS OF OLDER SPAIN

Germans or Flemings were her first preceptors in this craft. These artists had been sent for, or proceeded of their own accord, to Spain, and settling in this country rapidly spread the technics of their art among the Spaniards. In the Peninsula the origin of this school or movement may be traced to Burgos. Here, just as the fifteenth century was drawing to its close, and just before the breath of the Renaissance crossed the Spanish frontier at its eastern side, was gathered a small though influential group of eminent workers in more crafts than one ; painters and sculptors, architects, embroiderers, carvers of wood, *reja*-makers, and painters of cathedral glass. Prominent among them all was a foreigner named Philip Vigarny,[1] who is described by Diego de Sagrado as "singular above all others in the art of making statuary and sculpture ; a man of vast experience, general in his mastery of the liberal and mechanic arts, and no less resolute in all that is related with the sciences of architecture."

Burgundy is said to have been the birthplace of Felipe de Borgoña, but of his early history we

[1] In Spanish he is called Felipe de Borgoña, but Martí y Monsó says that the proper spelling of the surname is Biguerny.

70

XXX

70

DETAIL OF CHOIR-STALLS

(Convent of San Marcos, León)

FURNITURE

have no tidings. In documents which bear
his signature he styles himself "*imaginario*,
resident at Burgos." Three such documents
exist. On August 1st, 1505, he agrees, for 130,000
maravedis, to make "such images as may be
necessary" for the altar of the high chapel of
Palencia cathedral, "he with his own hand to
carve the hands and faces, out of good smooth
walnut, without painting." This document is
dated from Palencia. The other two are dated
severally, Burgos, December 6th, 1506, and
Corcos, September 6th, without the addition of
the year.[1] We also know this craftsman to have
made the great *retablo* of Burgos cathedral.
Such, from the fragmentary semblance we can
trace of him, was Philip Vigarny, the pioneer
of the wood-carvers of older Spain, and who,
aided by other craftsmen from abroad, communicated all the secrets of his art to Spaniards such
as Gil de Siloe, Ruy Sanchez, Diego de la Cruz,
Alonso de Lima, and Berruguete.

The typical *sillería* consists of two tiers; the
sellia or upper seats, with high backs and a canopy,
intended for the canons, and the lower seats or

---

[1] Zarco del Valle, *Documentos Inéditos para la Historia de las
Bellas Artes en España*, pp. 161, 162

71

subsellia, of simpler pattern and with lower backs, intended for the *beneficiados*. At the head of all is placed the presidential throne, larger than the other stalls, and covered, in many cases, by a canopy surmounted by a tall spire. When the *sillería* belongs to a monastery, the higher stalls are for the *profesos*, and the lower for the novices and *legos*. Commonly the part that forms the actual seat is hinged and rises to a vertical position, being so contrived that when the occupant rises to his feet, there remains a narrow ledge projecting from the under surface. This ledge is called the "seat of pity" or "of patience," because the worshipper is able to incline himself on it and give his limbs some measure of repose without appearing to be seated. There also is commonly another piece, intended for him to rest his hands upon in rising, which projects from the sides of the stall and forms a part of the decorative carving, as well as, somewhat higher still, the carved support to rest his arms while he is on his feet.

The earliest Spanish *sillerías* date from the fourteenth century; but it is not until the century succeeding that we find them at their very best. Gothic or Plateresco *sillerías* of marvellous design

XXXI

"SAMSON"

(Carved Choir-stall of Leon Cathedral

FURNITURE

and workmanship are those of the Seo of Zaragoza (begun in 1412), the Cartuja de Miraflores of Burgos (1489), the monastery of Oña, Santa María de Nájera (1495), the church of Santa María del Campo, in the province of Burgos, Santo Tomás of Avila (finished in 1493), and the cathedrals of Oviedo, Segovia (1461–1497), Ciudad Rodrigo, Tarragona (1478), Tarazona, Toledo (begun in 1494), Zamora, Astorga, Barcelona (1453–1483), and Seville (finished in 1478).

The Gothic choir-stalls of the Seo of Zaragoza have lofty backs with arabesque Mudejar ornamentation, small Gothic columns, and medallions containing figures upon the arms of every stall. The material is Flemish oak. The carving was begun in 1412 by the Moors Alí Arrondi, Muza, and Chamar, who earned a daily wage of four *sueldos*. In 1446 Juan Navarro and the brothers Antonio and Francisco Gomar were working at the same stalls, and also, in 1449, Francoy.

The stalls of the Cartuja de Miraflores at Burgos were carved by Martin Sánchez, who received in 1486, and for the *mano de obra* alone, the sum of 125,000 *maravedis*. The material, which was presented by Luis de Velasco, Señor of Belorado, is dark walnut.

The *sillería* of Santa María de Nájera, the work of Maestro Andrés and Maestro Nicolás, is Gothic merging into the Renaissance. That of Santo Tomás of Avila (late Gothic) consists of sixty oaken stalls, besides two larger ones resembling thrones (Plate xxiv.), intended to be occupied by Ferdinand and Isabella, founders of this monastery, and whose arms they bear in lace-like carving. The rest of the decoration is composed of thistles, vines, trefoils, and pomegranates. Owing to the fact that not a single cross appears on any part of the *sillería* (although this circumstance is not unusual in sacred Gothic woodwork), there is a superstition that these stalls were wrought anonymously by some Jew, condemned to execute them by the Inquisition as a form of punishment. This fable has no value. Although the author's name is not upon the stalls, they are identical in nearly every detail with those of the Cartuja de Miraflores at Burgos, known to have been carved by Martin Sánchez in 1486. Hence it is extremely probable that this craftsman was the author of both *sillerías*.

XXXII

74

"ESAU"

(Carved Choir-stall of León Cathedral)

FURNITURE

On many Spanish *sillerías* we find most spirited reproductions of the life and manners of their time; satirical allusions to contemporary vices, allegories and caprices as fantastic, in the phrase of Vargas Ponce, as "one of Bosch's nightmares," hunting-scenes or love-scenes, banquets, tournaments, dances, battles, sieges, and even bull-fights. Thus, on the stalls of the cathedrals of Zamora, Oviedo, Plasencia, Astorga, and León are carved such subjects as the following. A fox dressed as a friar, preaching to a group of hens but slyly abstracting their chicks (Zamora), men fighting with their fists (Zamora), a hog playing the bagpipes (León), the Devil in the garb of a confessor, tempting a penitent (León), a woman suckling an ass (León), a man armed with a lance, fighting a woman (Astorga), a bird of prey struggling with a crocodile (Astorga), card-players (Astorga), a warrior on all-fours, whipped by a woman (Plasencia), an *auto-de-fé* (Plasencia), swine praying and spinning (Ciudad Rodrigo), a fight between a tiger and a bull (Ciudad Rodrigo), a monkey beating a drum (Ciudad Rodrigo), and a monkey wearing a mitre (Ciudad Rodrigo).

The style of the lower stalls of Toledo cathedral

is good Plateresque. They were begun in 1494 by Maese Rodrigo, one of the very best of Spain's *entalladores*, and portray, in each successive stall, the phases of the last campaign against Granada (Plate xxv.); the sieges or battles of Altora, Melis, Xornas, Erefran, Alminia, Baza, Málaga (two stalls), Salobreña, Almuñecar, Comares, Beles, Montefrío, Moclín, Illora, Loja, Cazarabonela, Coyn, Cartama, Marbella, Ronda, Setenil, Alora, Alhama, Nixar, Padux, Vera, Huéscar, Guadix, Purchena, Almería, Rión, Castil de Ferro, Cambril, Zagani, Castul, Gor, Canzoria, Moxacar, Vélez el Blanco, Gurarca, Vélez el Rubio, Soreo, and Cabrera.

The upper tier of the same stalls belongs to a later period, and will, in consequence, be noticed subsequently.

The *sillería* of Barcelona cathedral was begun in the middle of the fifteenth century by Matias Bonafé, at the same time that the German Michael Locher and his pupil John Frederic worked at the canopies. It was finished thirty years later. Upon the back (which otherwise is plain) of every stall is a coat of arms distinct from all its neighbours, marking the seat of one of the princes or nobles summoned by Charles the

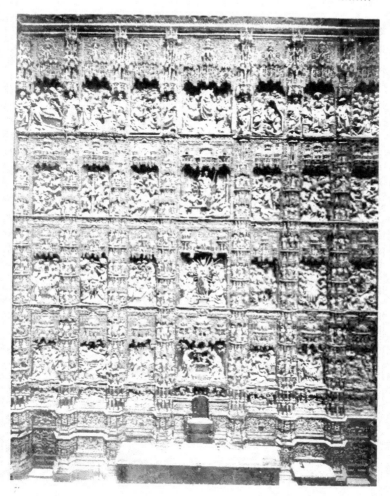

XXXIII

RETABLO
(Sevilla Catedral)

FURNITURE

Fifth to the Chapter of the Order of the Golden Fleece, March 5th, 1519.[1]

The splendid *sillería* of Seville cathedral is a mingling of the Gothic with the Mudejar and Plateresque. The material is oak and fir, and the number of the seats one hundred and seventeen. The *sellia* are surmounted by a graceful running *guardapolvo*. Each seat is carved distinctly from the rest, and further decorated in the Mudejar style with inlaid woods of various kinds and colours, imitating stone mosaic. Among this labyrinth of design are groups of people, angels, animals, and scenes from Scripture, as well as, on the lower stalls, the Giralda tower, which forms the arms of the cathedral. The *sillería* is further embellished with two hundred and sixteen statuettes, seventy-two of which are ranged along the canopy or *dosel*, the remainder being distributed between the seats.

The authors of this splendid work of art (judiciously restored some years ago by Boutelou, Fernandez, and Mattoni) were Nufio Sanchez, Dancart, and several other craftsmen, concerning

[1] "The stalls of the choir are neatly carved, and hung with escutcheons of princes and noblemen, among which I remarked the arms of our Henry the Eighth."—Swinburne.

77

whom we know but very little. Sánchez'
name is carved upon the second stall of the
upper row, and on the side of the Evangelist,
as follows :—

The above inscription states that "this choir
was made by Nufio Sanchez, *entallador* (God
guard him [1]), and finished in the year one thousand
four hundred and seventy-eight."

With the dawn of the sixteenth century, the
Gothic style runs rapidly into that of the Renaissance. At about this time, and as Baron Davillier
pointed out, we sometimes find a triple influence,
namely, the Burgundian, the Italian, and the native
Spanish. Vigarny may be called the champion

[1] This kind of parenthetical remark or prayer is one of the many
Muslim phrases that have passed into the regular service of the
Spanish Christian.

XXXIV

RETABLO OF SEVILLE CATHEDRAL.

(Detail of Carving)

of the first of these, Berruguete (who studied in Italy) of the second, and Guillermo Doncel of the third. After this the purer Renaissance gives place to the decadent, as in the stalls of Santiago, Málaga, Cordova, and Salamanca.

Sixteenth-century *sillerías* of note are those of Burgos cathedral (Plate xxvi.), carved by Vigarny, Avila cathedral, the Pilar of Zaragoza, the Minor Friars of the Cartuja of Burgos, Pamplona cathedral, San Marcos of León, Huesca, the *alta sillería* of Toledo, and the walnut stalls—carved in 1526 by Bartolomé Fernandez de Segovia, and now in the Madrid Museum—of the Parral of Segovia.

The *sillería* of Avila cathedral is believed to have been begun in 1527 by Juan Rodrigo, although the greater part of it was probably executed between 1536 and 1547 by Cornelis de Holanda, who took for his model the stalls of San Benito of Valladolid. The cost of the walnut wood and of its workmanship amounted to 33,669 *reales*.

The upper stalls of Toledo cathedral were carved by Vigarny and Alonso Berruguete in collaboration, so that we find in them the northern and Italian styles effectively and interestingly

79

united. The Plateresque-Renaissance *sillería*, described as " genuinely Spanish," of the old convent of San Marcos of León, containing statuettes of biblical personages and of fathers of the Church—Saint Isidore among them,—was finished in 1542 by Guillermo Doncel, who added the inscription "*Magister Guillermus Doncel me fecit MDXLII*" (Plate xxvii.). We know, however, nothing more about this excellent Spanish artist, except that (on the unsupported testimony of Cean) he worked at the façade of this convent between the years 1537 and 1544.

The intricate *sillería* of the Pilar of Zaragoza, containing almost every kind of subject—beasts, birds and fishes, allegories, incidents of the chase, or scenes of popular life—was designed by Esteban de Obray, a Navarrese, and executed by him and his assistants, Juan Moreto Florentino and Nicolas de Lobato, between 1542 and 1548. That of the Minor Friars of the Cartuja of Burgos was carved at a cost of eight hundred and ten ducats by Simón de Bueras, in 1558. That of Pamplona cathedral dates from about the middle of the century, and is the work of one Ancheta, who had visited Italy and gathered inspiration from the masterpieces of Siena. The material is English

XXXV

DETAIL OF *RETABLO*

(*Late 15th century. Museum of Valladolid*)

FURNITURE

oak. The stalls of Huesca, carved from oak proceeding from an older *sillería* which had been removed, were begun in 1587 and finished in 1594. The craftsmen were Nicolás de Verástegui and Juan Verrueta de Sangüesa.

Seventeenth-century *sillerías* are those of Santiago, carved by Juan de Vila in 1603; Salamanca, in 1651, by Alfonso Balbás; Orihuela, in 1692, by Juan Bautista Borja; and Segorbe, carved in the same year by Nicolás Camarón; while dating from the eighteenth century — a period of manifest decadence in this beautiful but short-lived craft—are the stalls of Lerida, by Luis Bonifar y Masó (born in 1730), and Cordova, executed between 1748 and 1757, at a cost of 913,889 *reales*, by Pedro Ciriaco Duque y Cornejo, a son of Seville and a pupil of the Sevillano Roldan.

The least imperfect of these later and decadent *sillerías* is that of Málaga, whose author, Pedro de Mena, was, like his master, Alonso Cano, a native of Granada.

Mena's contract with two canons of the cathedral, nominated by the bishop to prepare and sign the stipulations, will be found in No. 134 of the *Boletín de la Sociedad de Excursiones*.

The stalls of Málaga number a hundred and one, carved in walnut, larch, cedar, and the heavy Indian wood called *granadillo*. As happens with many of the *sillerías* of this country, the costumes of the figures are of great historical value. Among the saints is San Roque, in pilgrim's garb, attended by the dog who brought him day by day a loaf of bread while men refused to succour him.

No less magnificent than these sets of choir-stalls are the carved *retablos* or altar-screens,[1] a gradual excrescence from the primitive and un-pretentious altar of the early days of Christianity. Several kinds of craftsmen worked upon these altar-screens, such as *tallistas, entalladores, imagineros*, and even architects.

The Golden Age of the *retablo* embraces the end of the fifteenth century and the whole of the sixteenth. Notable examples belonging to this

[1] Wood is the usual material for these altar-screens, though sometimes marble was employed, or stone, or silver. Of Genoese marble is the *retablo* (end of the fourteenth or beginning of the fifteenth century) of the Cartuja del Paular in the Lozoya valley ; of stone, those of the parish church of San Nicolás at Burgos (end of the fifteenth or beginning of the sixteenth century), and of the "chapel of the tailors" in Tarragona Cathedral ; while a silver *retablo*, in the Renaissance style, was that of the church, now demolished, of Santa María at Madrid.

XXXVI

82

DETAIL OF *RETABLO*

(Chapel of Santa Ana, Burgos Cathedral)

FURNITURE

period are the screens of the monastery of Santo
Tomás at Avila, San Martin of Segovia, the
Cartuja de Miraflores, the Colegiata of Covarrubias in the province of Burgos, the cathedrals
of Avila, Toledo, Tudela, and Tarazona; several
in the churches of Toledo, two in the church of
San Lesmes (Burgos), two in Burgos Cathedral
(Plate xxxvi.), and three, including those of *Reyes*
and of *Buena Mariana*, in the church of San Gil
in the same city. Not one of these, however,
has the grandeur or variety of the altar-screen
of Seville (Plates xxxiii. and xxxiv.), which is
carefully described in Cean's monograph. "The
style is Gothic; the material, undecaying larch;
and the screen, which reaches nearly to the
vaulting, is the largest in the country, although
at first it spanned the presbytery only, not
including either side. It was designed in 1482
by Dancat or Danchart, who began work upon
it as soon as his sketches were approved, and
worked at it till 1492, in which year he seems to
have died.

"Dancat was succeeded by Master Marco and
Bernardo de Ortega, whose carving reached, by
1505, the canopy or *viga*, and who were followed
in their turn by Francisco, Bernardo's son, father

83

and teacher of Bernardino and Nufrio de Ortega, his assistants. Some of the statues were carved by Micer Domingo. The rest of the *imaginería* was finished in 1526 ; and the gilding and painting were done by Alejo Fernández, his brother, and Andrés de Covarrubias.

"So the screen remained till 1550, when the Chapter decided to extend it, without altering the style of decoration, to the sides of the presbytery. By this time Spanish sculpture had improved, and many of our best-known sculptors lent their aid, of whom the earliest were Roque Balduc, Pedro Becerril, el Castellano, Juan de Villalva, Diego Vazquez, and Pedro Bernal. In 1553 the Chapter appointed, to inspect the work of these artists, Juan Reclid and Luis de Aguilar, both of whom lived at Jaen. Henceforth the master-craftsmen working at the screen were Pedro de Heredia, Gomez de Orozco, Diego Vazquez the younger, Juan Lopez, Andrés Lopez del Castillo, and his sons, Juan de Palencia, and Juan Bautista Vazquez. By 1564 the screen was quite concluded.

"The Gothic work is of incomparable richness. Ten groups of tall and narrow columns, resting upon two pedestals or socles, divide the *retablo* into nine spaces, crossed by horizontal bands of complicated carving, forming a series of thirty-six niches, in four rows. Statues a little less than life-size represent, in the first row, the creation and fall of our first parents, and the mysteries of the infancy of Christ ; in the second, His preaching and miracles ; in the third, His passion and death ; and in the fourth, His resurrection, appearance to the disciples, and ascension ; also the coming of the Holy Ghost. Upon the altar-table, and resting in its niche, is the statue, covered with silver plates, of Nuestra Señora de la Sede, presented to this temple by Saint Ferdinand. Above the *viga*, which has an *artesonado* ceiling, rises a frontispiece containing thirteen canopied niches with statues of the apostles, and in the centre niche that of the Virgin Mary. Crowning the whole *retablo* are statues larger than life-size, and a Calvary standing in free space."[1]

Throughout these Spanish altar-screens the influence which predominates is that of Germany. They are essentially distinguished by a Northern art (Plates xxxv., xxxvi.), not sentimental but material, not tender but robust, not (like the art of the Italians) retrospective or prospective, but prosaic,

[1] *Descripción de la Catedral de Sevilla*, pp. 27, 28.

realistic, actual. Curiously enough, their presence seems incongruous in Spain, and yet they made themselves at home here; for Spanish art was ever realistic, so probably on this account two widely different nations found, at least in this particular craft, a common bond of sympathy. Certainly the Renaissance, while it seemed to cherish and encourage, really undermined and killed this branch of Spanish wood-carving. A similar phenomenon attends the art of the Alhambra. In either case the plenitude of power and of beauty is even more ephemeral than the term of human life; and thus, deluded by so brilliant and majestic a decay, we fail to apprehend, or seek to grow oblivious of, the imminence of their ruin.

Ivories

IVORIES

THE story of Spanish ivory-work is shortly told, for probably no craft, excepting glass, has been so little practised in this country. The older Spanish writers rarely mention it, although from time to time this substance may have been employed for carving diptyches and boxes, and Roderick is stated to have entered the battle of the Guadalete in an ivory car, by which is meant, perhaps, a chariot of Byzantine make or pattern, covered with ivory plates. However, properly speaking, the history of this art as exercised in Spain begins in the eleventh century, attains its prime towards the fourteenth century, and ceases altogether at the time of the Renaissance.

Among the ivory objects now preserved in Spain, and which were wrought by artists other than Mohammedan, none is more interesting or important than the consular diptych of Oviedo cathedral. Although this valuable diptych was not made in Spain, but manifests Byzantine art in all its purity, it well deserves to be described. It consists of two ivory tablets measuring sixteen inches and a half in height by twelve inches and a half across both leaves. Each leaf has a simple border of a triple form, and just inside each corner is a circular floral ornament in relief, with a lion's head in the centre. Another ornament, also circular, is in the centre of each leaf, and contains, carved within a graceful S-shaped border, a half-length portrait of the Consul, who is represented in the act of throwing down into the amphitheatre his *mappa* or handkerchief[1] with his right hand, while in his left he holds the sceptre (*scipio imaginifer*), crowned with a small bust. His hair is curled in the Byzantine fashion, and his costume is a richly decorated toga.

An inscription runs along the top of either tablet, between the border and the circular devices carved with flowers. It says :—

Flavius Strategius Apion—Strategius Apion. Vir inlustris Comes Devotissimorum Domesticorum et Consul ordinarius.

---

[1] *I.e.* as a signal to begin the sport. The same usage (except that the handkerchief is waved, and not thrown down) is followed at this moment in the Spanish bull-ring.

IVORIES

We gather, therefore, that this magnate was a chamberlain at court, as well as ordinary consul.

Diptyches were used among the Romans for all kinds of purposes, such as to convey love-messages, as invitations to a banquet, or to notify the celebration of feasts and games. We find the diptych also used in Christian temples from the time of Constantine, serving to record church festivals or names of saints and martyrs, as covers for a copy of the gospel (*diptycha evangeliorum*), or as reliquaries (*thecae reliquiarum*). Sometimes these diptyches were wrought expressly for the church, or sometimes they were consular diptyches that had been preserved from former ages. This latter class, when cleansed from pagan usage and devoted to the ceremonies of the Christian faith, was known as *diptycha mixta*.

Such early objects as were wrought in ivory by Spanish hands, consisting as a rule of circular or oblong, square or oval caskets, were principally carved by Moors or Mudejares. Among the Spanish-Moorish boxes which are still preserved are several of the greatest interest and beauty (Plates xxxviii., xxxix., xl.). One of them, made from pieces of an older casket believed to date from earlier than the Moorish conquest, is in the National Museum. The decoration in its present form consists of Arabic inscriptions in relief, together with figures of the apostles. This casket, which proceeds from the Colegiata of Saint Isidore at León, measures seven inches in length by five in depth and six in height, and has been used as a reliquary.

Another, dating from the middle of the eleventh century and proceeding from the same temple as the one just noticed, is also in the National Museum. It was a present from the Emir Mohammed Almotamid-Aben-Abed to his second wife, Al-Badir ("the Moon"), and includes among the decoration dogs and doves, symbolic of affection and fidelity. The style of carving is what is known as Persian-Arabic. We do not know, however, whether the box was imported from the East, or whether it was made in Spain by somebody of Persian parentage or skilled in Persian art. The material is a delicate *taracea* of sandal, aloe, and cypress woods inlaid on larch. The box, which was used at León as a reliquary, has bronze clasps, and is inscribed along the top with sentences from which we learn that it was made by Aben-As-Serag.

In the cathedral of Pamplona is a magnificent

XXXVIII

IVORY CASKET

(Obverse: 11th Century. Pamplona Cathedral)

ivory box (Plate xxxviii.) which was originally at
Sangüesa in Navarre. It measures, says Riaño,
fifteen inches long by nine and a quarter inches
wide. "It is completely covered with carvings
in relief, within circular cusped medallions, with
figures in the centres representing different
subjects; men seated, hawking, or struggling
with wild beasts, and numerous single figures of
lions, stags, and other animals. The intermediate
spaces contain an ornamentation of leaves and
flowers which is accommodated to the geometrical
style of Saracenic art. Round the upper part of
this box appears an Arabic inscription in fine
Cufic characters :—'In the name of God. The
blessing of God, the complete felicity, the happi-
ness, the fulfilment of the hope of good works,
and the adjourning the fatal period (of death), be
with the Hagib Seifo daula (sword of the State),
Abdelmalek ben Almansur. This (box) was made
by the orders (of the said Hagib), under the in-
spection or direction of his chief eunuch, Nomayr
ben Mohammad Alaumeri, his slave, in the year
of 395 (A.D. 1005).'

"In the centre medallion, on the opposite side
to the lock, is represented the standing figure of
a man who is attacked by two lions. He holds

on his arm a shield, upon which is engraved an
inscription, with the following religious formula :
' There is no god but God,' or a similar one,
for the characters are very illegible and confused.
In the centre of this shield may be read the words,
' Made by Hair,' undoubtedly one of the artists
who made the box. Another artist's name may
be read with difficulty in a similar inscription
which appears on one of the medallions on the
left side ; it is written on the thigh of a stag,
which is attacked by a lion : ' It was made by
Obeidat.' Three other inscriptions of a similar
character appear in other parts of this box, which
probably give the names of other artists, but I
have been unable to decipher them."

Other interesting boxes dating from the same
period are that of Santo Domingo de Silos at
Burgos, and several which are in the National
Museum at Madrid. The box which is preserved
at Burgos is made of ivory, and measures thirteen
inches and a quarter in length by seven inches
and a half in width and height. The decorative
work consists of hunting scenes, and also of an
inscription in Cufic characters which says : " Permanent felicity for the owner (of this box). May
God lengthen his days. It was made at Medina

XXXIX

IVORY BOX

(11th Century. *Palencia Cathedral*)

IVORIES

. . .[1] in the year four hundred and seventeen (A.D. 1025). It is the work of his servant Mohammed-ibn-Zeiyan. May God glorify him."

There is also in the provincial museum of Burgos a handsome ivory diptych which was formerly at the convent of Santo Domingo de Silos. It bears at each extremity—that is, four times repeated—the following inscription :—" This was ordered to be made by the Iman, servant of God, Abd-er-Rhaman, prince of believers."

Among the rectangular boxes in the National Museum is one of carved ivory, with an inscription recording it to have been a gift from Prince Ali to one of the favourites of his harem, and another of the same material which was once upon a time at Carrion de los Condes, in the province of Palencia. This box is painted with a decorative pattern in carmine and dark green. The lid, which is imperfect, contains the following inscription in Cufic characters, standing boldly out against a green ground :—" In the name of Allah, the Merciful, the Compassionate. The protection of Allah and an impending victory for the servant of Allah . . . and his wali Maad

[1] At this break in the inscription Riaño professed to discover the beginning of the word *Cuenca.*

Abu-Temim—the Iman Al-Moez . . . prince of believers (the blessing of Allah be upon him and his sons the good). (This) was commanded to be made for (celebrating) the fortunate victory. It was made by . . . Jorasani." The length of this box is eighteen inches, and its height nine inches.

A fine Moorish box (Plate xxxix.), now in the cathedral of Palencia, is covered with elaborately engraved and perforated ivory plates upon a ground of gilt leather backed by wood, and further ornamented with enamel-work upon a copper surface. This box is fourteen inches long, and has a gable top. The decoration on the sides and lid consists of palm-leaves, birds, and men engaged in combating and chasing antelopes and lions in the characteristic manner of Assyrian art. A lengthy Cufic inscription tells us that the box was made at Cuenca (*Medina Cuenca*) by Abd-er-Rahman ben Ziyan, to the order of the Moorish princes of Toledo, and that it dates from the year 441 of the Hegira.[1] Vives has pointed out that Cuenca was evidently

[1] Detailed accounts of this casket will be found in the *Boletín de la Sociedad Española de Excursiones* for June 1893, and in the *Boletín de la Real Academia de la Historia*, vol. xx.

XL

HISPANO-MORESQUE IVORY CASKET

(13th Century. Royal Academy of History, Madrid)

a principal centre of this industry, and that caskets executed here about this time exist in Perpignan cathedral and in the provincial museum of Burgos.

Riaño mentions seven ivory boxes of particular interest, which were probably made in Spain by Spanish Arabs, or else by Eastern craftsmen who had emigrated to this country. "On all their carving," he adds, "the names of Spanish historical persons appear, and it is hardly possible that they were ordered in remote countries, especially as some of these objects are small and comparatively unimportant."

Two of these boxes are in the South Kensington Museum. The one which is cylindrical in shape and has a domed cover is thus described by Maskell in his *Ivories, Ancient and Mediæval, in the South Kensington Museum* :—" This beautiful box is carved throughout, except the bottom of it, with interlacing narrow bands forming quatrefoils, in which, on the cover, are four eagles. These have spread wings and stand erect ; well designed and most delicately executed. A small knob serves to lift the lid.

" Round the side, each quatrefoil is filled with a star having a leaf ornament. The same decoration is repeated in the spaces between the larger quatre-foils on the cover.

" The whole is carved in pierced work, except a band which forms the upper upright portion of the box, round the side of the lid. This band has an Arabic inscription : ' A favour of God to the servant of God, Al Hakem al Mostanser Billah, commander of the faithful.' He was a Caliph who reigned at Cordova, A.D. 961–976."

The other box is oblong and rectangular. " The cover and sides are carved with scroll foliated ornament ; the hinges and clasp are of chased silver inlaid with niello. Round the sides, immediately below the lid, is the following Arabic inscription in Cufic characters :—' In the name of God. This (box) was ordered to be made by Seidat Allah, the wife of Abd-er-Rahman, prince of the believers. God be merciful and satisfied with him.' " This inscription, adds Riaño, "must allude to Abd-er-Rahman the Third, the first Caliph of Cordova who bore the title of Emir, el Mumenin. The formula ' God be merciful,' etc., denotes that he was dead when it was written. He died A.D. 961."

Another Spanish-Moorish casket, also at South Kensington, and dating from the eleventh century,

IVORY CRUCIFIX

(11th Century. Madrid Museum)

IVORY CRUCIFIX

(11th Century. Back view. Madrid Museum)

IVORIES

is described by Maskell as "richly carved in deep relief with foliage and animals in scrolls interlacing one another, and forming larger and smaller circles. The top and each side is a single plaque of ivory ; the sloping lid at the front and back has two panels. On the two are two animals, like doves ; a large bird stands at the back of each, attacking it with his beak. The sloping sides have, in the large circles, men on horseback, and animals fighting. The intermediate spaces are completely filled with foliage, and smaller beasts. Similar subjects are repeated in the circles on the panels forming the lower sides of the casket, and among them are two groups of men and women sitting ; one blowing a horn, another playing on a guitar, another holding a cup in one hand and a flower in the other." Riaño adds : " There is no inscription on this casket, but in one of the medallions on the lid there is a bust, which is carried on the back of a horse, and which is probably a representation of the prince for whom the casket was made."

The *Letter of Testament* setting forth the various objects bequeathed by Ferdinand the First and his consort Sancha to the church of Saint John the Baptist (or of Saint Isidore) at

León, mentions an ivory cross (which will be noticed presently), an ivory box fitted with gold, and two ivory boxes fitted with silver, one of them containing three other silver boxes, similarly decorated.

One of these boxes is described by Ambrosio de Morales, and from his words we conclude it to be the one which was adorned with gold, "of which metal," he wrote in 1572, "it has even more than of ivory," adding that it measured more than half a yard in length, and enshrined the body of Saint Vincent of Avila. He also tells us that it bore the following inscription, carved upon a golden frieze :—

ARCULA SANCTORUM MICAT HAEC SUB HONORE DUORUM

BAPTISTAE SANCTI JOHANNIS SIVE PELAGII

CEU REX FERNANDUS, REGINAQUE SANTIA, FIERI JUSSIT.

ERA MILLENA SEPTENA SEU NONAGENA.[1]

This *arca* has been much mutilated, and stripped of all the precious metal. Morales' description is therefore of especial value, as are the ivory tablets (eleventh century), carved with Christian

[1] A.D. 1059.

XLII

BYZANTINE CRUCIFIX

themes, which yet remain upon the body of the box.

Dating from the thirteenth century is a Moorish casket (Plate xl.), preserved in the Academy of History at Madrid, and proceeding from the Carthusian monastery of Val de Cristo at Segorbe. It measures a foot in length by eight inches in height and four and a half inches in depth. The lid is deeply bevelled, and contains on each of the bevelled sides shields with the bars which constitute the arms of Aragon, painted upon a gold ground, together with imperial eagles painted in black upon a carmine ground. A decorative device of leaves and stems is also painted on the ivory.

Rodrigo Amador de los Ríos believes that this casket was captured in war by Jayme the First of Aragon, remaining with successive princes of his line until the reign of Don Martin, by whom it was presented to the monastery. The shields would thus be added to the primitive Moorish casket by some Christian - Spanish painter.

The ivory crucifix (Plates xli. and xli. (a)), of Ferdinand the First and Doña Sancha, made in the first half of the eleventh century, and offered by these sovereigns to the church of Saint John the Baptist (or of Saint Isidore) at León, measures twenty-one inches in length by thirteen inches and a half in height. The figure of Christ recalls the rigidness and rudeness of Byzantine craftsmanship, such as is found in ancient crucifixes still preserved in Spain (Plate xlii.). The pupils of the enormous, expressionless eyes are made of jet. We see the wound upon each foot, with wavy marks to imitate the flowing blood, but no trace of a nail. Nails, however, transfix the hands. The arms are separate from the trunk, but the *suppedaneum* on which the feet are resting is of a single piece with the body of the figure.

The surface of the cross, especially about the borders, contains elaborate decoration, including animals and foliage. Above the Saviour's head is the inscription :—

IHS NAZA

RENVS REX

IVDEORVM

Above this is another figure of Christ seated, crowned with a cruciform nimbus and holding a Greek processional cross. Beneath the feet of the larger figure is Adam in an uncouth posture,

XLIII

"THE VIRGIN OF BATTLES"

(13th Century, Seville Cathedral)

turning his head to gaze upward, and at the lower extremity of the cross are carved the words :—

FERDINANDVS REX

SANCIA REGINA

The lateral arms are carved with numerous devices forming an effective whole, including animals upon a tessellated band which seems to imitate a groundwork of mosaic. Other subjects represented are the Resurrection of the Flesh, the ascent of the blessed to Heaven, and the fall of the wicked to Hell.

Upon the obverse side are pairs of quadrupeds, birds, and serpents, among a maze of foliage, together with the eagle, lion, lamb, and ox, as symbols of the evangelists. The lion and the ox have wings, and at the foot of the cross is an angel.

The carving of the Saviour's form is clearly inferior to that of the decoration which surrounds it. Amador de los Ríos seeks to account for this by declaring that "the difficulty from the point of view of art increases in proportion as the size of the figure is required to be larger"—a statement with which I wholly disagree. I believe, in fact, that in this cross the figure of Christ and the surrounding ornamentation are not by the same hand, and that the carver of the decorative detail was simply the better craftsman of the two.

Many of the statuettes of the Virgin which are preserved in Spain were probably made in France. One that is typically and unquestionably Spanish is the celebrated "Virgin of Battles" (Plate xliii.), now guarded, together with other relics of Saint Ferdinand (see Vol. I. Plate xi.), in the Chapel Royal of Seville cathedral. These statuettes, the use of which originated with the Greek emperors, and which were called by the Byzantines *socia belli*, consist of a seated figure of the Virgin with a small door opening underneath her throne, and served as reliquaries, and also as a kind of talisman. Boutelou says that the Spanish warriors of the Middle Ages were accustomed to carry these images to war with them, fitted upon a pin protruding from the left side of the saddle-bow. The "Virgin of Battles," made in Spain in the early part of the thirteenth century, was thus carried by King Ferdinand the Saint, resting between his shield or *rodela* and his left arm, and so protected, and protecting, in the brunt of war.

The image is of ivory, and measures seventeen inches in height. The style is primitive Gothic,

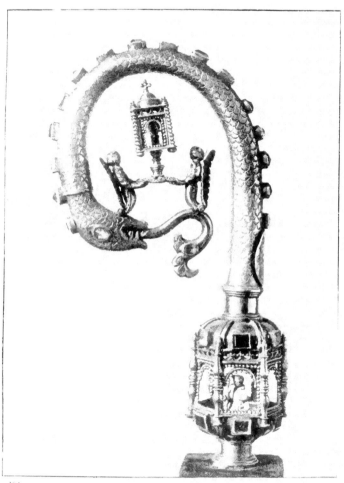

XLIV

SPANISH MEDIEVAL *BACULUS*

not as yet emancipated from Romanic and Byzantine art; and the expression of the Madonna and
her Babe is marked by an engaging sweetness.
Through lapse of centuries, myriads of diminutive
cracks have opened on the surface of the ivory,
and this has turned, in colour, to a brightish
yellow. The right arm of the Virgin was broken
off at some time prior to the sixteenth century,
and has been replaced by another one. Mother
and Child wear crowns of silver-gilt which probably were added later, and the hair, lips, and
eyes have been badly painted or repainted with
discordant colouring. A four-sided hole bored
deep into the ivory served for holding the image
to the *perno* which projected from the monarch's
saddle-bow.

A few elaborate *baculi* or pastoral staves
(Plate xliv.) exist in Spain, including one of the
fourteenth century, in ivory, which belonged to the
late Marquis of Monistrol, and is carved with the
Crucifixion and also with the Virgin contemplating
the Holy Infant as He is offered cups by angels.
Another interesting Spanish baculus, though not
of ivory, but copper decorated with turquoises and
bright blue enamel, belonged to Bishop Pelayo
de Cebeyra of Mondoñedo (A.D. 1199–1218), and

has been preserved, together with that prelate's gilded shoes. In the celebrated processions of Santiago, at which Alfonso the Sixth was personally present, magnificent ivory *baculi* were borne, not only by the archbishop (*eburnea virga ponti-ficali decoratus*), but even by the choristers.

Between the eleventh and the fifteenth centuries, Spanish craftsmen produced a fair quantity of ivory boxes, reliquaries, diptyches, triptyches, combs, and other less important objects. A fifteenth-century ivory spoon, ten inches long, whose handle is carved with six crocodiles, is in the National Museum, and may be Spanish work. In the same collection are one or two ivory diptyches and leaves of diptyches, and a wooden box (fourteenth century), with figures of carved ivory representing passages from the life of Saint George upon the body of the box, and from the Old Testament upon the lid. A carved Renaissance temple of the same material, with the Virgin and Child in its interior, is probably Italian.

In the fortieth volume of *España Sagrada* it is stated that four ivory diptyches (*quatuor dictacos eburneos*) were offered in A.D. 897 to Lugo cathedral by Alfonso the Third and his queen Jimena. Other ivory diptyches were presented

in A.D. 1063 by Ferdinand the Second to the church of Saint Isidore at León. José Villaamil, in his study of an ivory statuette of the Virgin, belonging to the nuns of Allariz (*Boletín de la Sociedad Española de Excursiones*; nos. 76 and 77), mentions a carved ivory box (*capsa eburnea*) made in the year 1122 for Santiago cathedral by order of Archbishop Gelmirez; another which existed in the sixteenth century in the church of Santa María at Finisterre; and a third, used as a reliquary, which in 1572 was opened by the monks of Samos in presence of Ambrosio de Morales.

During the Middle Ages portable altars (*altares portátiles*) were widely used in Spain, and some were made of ivory. It was the custom to open them at the time of prayer, and as a rule they rested upon *reclinatorios* or hung upon the wall. The *imagen abriente* or "opening image" was also popular in Spain throughout the twelfth and thirteenth centuries. As the name implies, these images opened in the manner of a triptych, and were very often used as reliquaries. Specimens are preserved in many parts of Europe, but only one or two exist in Spain and Portugal. That which belongs to the nuns of Allariz dates from the end of the thirteenth century, and was a present from Queen Violante. It is described fantastically by Morales, and accurately by Villa-amil, but the quaintest account is by the chronicler Jacobo de Castro. It measures, Castro tells us, "about half-a-yard in length and is one of the fairest ever seen, since it opens downward from the neck, discovering, on plates of half-relief, the principal mysteries of Christ and of Our Lady. The devotion towards it of the people in this neighbourhood exceeds description, and God has wrought a quantity of miracles through the intercession thereof."

A fourteenth-century triptych carved in bone with scenes from Scripture is in the National Museum. It proceeds from Aragon, and is said to have belonged to Jayme the Conqueror. The Escorial possesses a handsome ivory diptych (Plate xlvi.) which is either Spanish or Italian— probably the former. It measures exactly a foot in height by nine inches across both leaves, and is deeply carved with passages from the life of Christ. The style is late Romanic merging into Gothic, and points to the second half of the thirteenth century.

Pottery

POTTERY

ANCIENT

QUANTITIES of ancient common pottery have been, and are continually being found in many parts of Spain. Prehistoric cups, shaped with the fingers and dried and hardened by the sun, are preserved in the Museum of History at Barcelona. They were discovered at Argar. Similar objects have been extracted from the caves of Segóbriga, Lóbrega in Old Castile, and El Tesoro in the province of Málaga. Those which were found at Segóbriga are divided by Capelle into six groups, one of which includes a vessel resembling the ordinary Spanish pitcher of to-day.

Villa-amil y Castro has described in the *Museo Español de Antigüedades* pieces of prehistoric sun-dried ware discovered in Galicia, roughly decorated with patterns imprinted by the finger. In other instances a double spiral has been described with a pointed instrument about the vessel's neck. Similar fragments have been found by Góngora in Andalusia. Celtic pottery was found in 1862 by Captain Brome on Windmill Hill at Gibraltar, in 1866 by M. Lartet in the caves of Torrecilla de Cameros, and by Casiano de Prado in a cave near Pedraza, as well as at Navares de Ayuso and elsewhere. In central Spain, vessels of the Celtiberian era have been found in tombs at Prádena, and pieces of red Saguntine ware, with dark red decoration, at Otero de Herreros, close to vestiges of a Roman mine. Lecea y García describes in his work on *Old Segovian Industries* a Celtiberian plate of reddish clay covered with black varnish, which was dug up some years ago in a garden at that town. This plate, measuring no less than four feet in diameter, and containing two inscriptions in characters believed to be Celtiberian, as well as the figure of a warrior armed with a lance and three javelins, was submitted to Heiss, who wrote of it in the *Gazette Archéologique* and pronounced it to be genuine. I have not seen the plate in question. I have, however, met with cleverly executed forgeries, also varnished black, of primitive Spanish pottery.

POTTERY

In 1899 quantities of Celtic ware, believed to date from the time of the Phœnicians, or even earlier, were unearthed by M. Bonsor from tumuli in the Guadalquivir valley. These objects are ornamented in relief with complicated patterns paler than the ground, obtained by using lighter-coloured clay. "As similar Celtic pottery has been found in Portugal, it will be understood that the Celtic influence, having crossed the Pyrenees, reached the south by the western seaboard. It will thus be seen that long before the arrival of the Romans a relatively high degree of civilisation had been reached at least in the south of Spain."[1]

In the summer of 1905 two German archæologists, Messrs. Schulten and Könen, who had obtained permission from the Spanish Government to explore the site of old Numancia, filled four large cases with the Celtiberian pottery they extracted from the ruins. These cases were forwarded to the University of Göttingen. I understand, however, that they have been returned, or are to be returned immediately, to Spain.

Long before the Christian era, Greek colonies existed on the Spanish coast at Rhodas, Denia,

[1] Martin Hume, *The Spanish People*, p. 15 (note).

Emporium (Ampurias), Saguntum (Murviedro), and elsewhere. Pottery of good design and workmanship was manufactured at these towns, and strongly influenced native art. Bowls and other objects showing such an influence were discovered by M. Bonsor in his recent excavations. Another powerful influence was that of Rome. Roman potteries existed in the suburb of Seville called Triana, and in the provinces of Cáceres and Badajoz. Mérida was also an important centre of this industry, and vessels which were used in sacred rites, such as the *aquiminarium*, the *prefericulum*, the *simpulum*, and the *urnula*, were discovered here not long ago. The name "Saguntine ware" was given by the Romans to a kind of pottery which seems to have been made along the Spanish littoral extending southward from Saguntum. Fragments of this pottery, which closely resembles the Arezzo ware,[1] are

[1] "A ware exactly like that of Arezzo, called by some the red Roman ware, and by others Samian, distinguished by its close grain composed of a fine clay, and presenting, when broken, edges of an opaque light red colour, whilst the inner and outer surfaces are quite smooth, and of a brighter and darker red, is found in all places of the ancient world to which the Roman arms or civilisation reached. It is distinguished from the Aretine by its darker tone, stronger glaze, and coarser ornamentation. Possibly, the whole passage of Pliny in which he speaks of the earthenware of his day refers to this

POTTERY

found in shoals upon the sites of Roman towns, particularly Tarragona. These *barros saguntinos*, or (as Hübner prefers to call them) *barros tarraconenses*, have been divided into four classes, namely, white, grey, red (covered with a dark red varnish),[1] and yellow striped with red. This ware is commonly adorned with garlands, animals, hunting - scenes, divinities, games, or religious ceremonies, and also bears, in nearly every case, the potter's name or mark; *e.g.* ALBINVS F ("Albinus fecit") or OF. ALBIN ("officina Albini"). More than two hundred marks have been discovered which were used by potters of Ampurias alone.

red ware. Thus, for dishes he praises the Samian and the Aretine ware ; for cups, that of Surrentum, Asta and Pollentia, Saguntum and Pergamus. Tralles and Mutina had their manufactories. Cos was most esteemed ; Hadria produced the hardest ware. That one of these, that of Saguntum, was a red ware, is clear ; that of Cumæ was also of the same colour. . . . That the red ware is found amidst the dense forests of Germany and on the distant shores of Britain, is a remarkable fact in the civilisation of the old world. It was apparently an importation, being exactly identical wherever discovered, and is readily distinguished from the local pottery."— Birch, *History of Ancient Pottery*, pp. 560, 561.

[1] "It belongs to the class of tender lustrous pottery, consisting of a bright red paste like sealing-wax, breaking with a close texture, and covered with a siliceous, or, according to some, a metallic glaze. This glaze is exceedingly thin, transparent, and equally laid upon the whole surface, only slightly augmenting the colour of the clay."— Birch, p. 561.

ARTS AND CRAFTS OF OLDER SPAIN

There seems to be no doubt that Saguntum and Emporium were principal centres of this industry, and possibly, since these towns were old Greek settlements, the *barros saguntinos* were of Grecian origin. Pella y Forgas, describing in his *History of the Ampurdan* the fine red ware of this locality, says that parts of the decoration were fashioned on the wheel, others directly by the potter's hand, and others from a mould, while the ornament of dotted lines was made by the wheeled *roulette*.

Among the commoner objects dating from this time are amphoræ and small earthen lamps (Pl. xlvii.). These lamps have been discovered in great numbers, and, owing to the dryness of the Spanish soil, in excellent preservation. They measure about the size of the hand, and have two holes, one in the spout or beak, to hold the wick, and the other at the top, for pouring in the oil. The top, which as a rule is slightly concave, is often ornamented with devices in relief, such as a chariot and its driver, or the emblem of a deity.

The typical amphora was a long, narrow vessel (usually of earthenware ; less frequently of brass or glass), with an elongated handle at either side of the neck, and tapering nearly to a point. It

XLVII

AMPHORAIC VASES AND OTHER POTTERY

(Museum of Cairo, 1901)

served for storing honey, oil, or wine, and in order
to keep it upright the pointed lower end was
stuck into the soil, or rested on a perforated
wooden stand. In the spring of 1893 some fisher-
men drew up in their nets, just off the coast of
Alicante, three large intact amphoræ thickly cased
with shells, and sold them for eight dollars each.
Other fine amphoræ, now in the collection of the
Marquis of Cerralbo, were washed upon the
beach at Torrevieja, and many more are in
museums. Vessels of this kind are known to
have been made at Rhodas (Rosas) and Saguntum,
and their use continued in Spain until the downfall of the second empire.

HISPANO-MORESQUE NON-LUSTRED POTTERY

The statements of Saint Isidore, confirmed
by one or two discoveries in southern Spain,
prove that the pottery in use among the Visigoths
was principally Roman. Probably in this, as in so
many of her arts, the Moorish conquest brought
about a radical and rapid change. Remains of
pottery dating from this period are extremely
rare. The provincial museum of Granada con-

tains some bowls and plates, all more or less imperfect, which are ascribed by experts to about the year 1000. These objects, which were dug up in 1878 on the slopes of the Sierra Elvira, a few miles from Granada, are coloured black and green upon a white or whitish ground. The most important is a dish which measures fourteen inches in diameter, and is decorated with a falcon on a horse's back (Plate xlviii.).[1] All of this pottery shows the double influence of Byzantium and the East. Among the designs upon the other pieces are hares and stags surrounded by a bordering of primitive arabesques. Riaño remarks that "it is almost impossible to assert whether this pottery was made in or imported into Spain." Nevertheless, Persians are stated to have settled in this region early in the days of Muslim rule, while these dilapidated specimens of ancient ware are greatly similar in colouring and substance to the common dishes and *barreños* which are still produced throughout the province of Granada.

Moorish potteries producing lustred or non-

---

[1] The falcon is one of the commonest devices on all Persian pottery, and was, in fact, the national emblem of the chase. Its importance for the purpose of pursuing and securing game is well described in Sir John Malcolm's *Sketches in Persia.*

XLVIII

About A.D. 1200. Museum of Granada

POTTERY

lustred ware existed from an early date at Málaga, Valencia, Toledo, Calatayud, Murviedro, Murcia, and Barcelona. Another centre of this craft was probably Granada ; for though she is not mentioned in this sense by any of the Moorish authors, the late Señor Contreras discovered here the vestiges of two ancient potteries, while one of the old entrances was known as Bab Alfajjarin, or "the potters' gate."

The Ordinances of Granada contain provisions which were evidently copied from the Spanish Moors, relating to the *almadraveros* or tilemakers, the *tinajeros* or makers of *tinajas*, and the *olleros* or potters generally. The Ordinances which concern the tilemakers are dated between 1528 and 1540. The restrictions imposed upon these craftsmen were irksome, foolish, and unnecessary. All bricks and tiles were to be stamped in three places with the city mark, and were only permitted to be made between the first of April and the thirty-first of October in each year, "since what is made at other seasons is not good or perfect, owing to the rain, and cold, and frost."

Another Ordinance, illustrating the lawlessness prevailing at Granada in the times succeeding the reconquest, complains that "many persons, in-

cluding labourers and hodmen, go forth into the
roads and streets, and seize the tiles and bricks
by violence from those who are conveying them,
and bear them to their houses, or to the work
which they are paid to do."

A picturesque, though cheap and unluxurious,
vessel of a thoroughly eastern character, and
which was very largely manufactured by the
Spanish Moors, is the terra-cotta *tinaja* or
gigantic jar for storing wine, or olive oil, or grain
(Plate xlix.). The use of these receptacles extended through the whole Peninsula, and has continued undiminished to this day. The principal
centres of *tinaja*-making were Toledo, Seville,
and Granada. The Ordinances of the latter town
embody Moorish rules relating to this branch
of pottery. These laws, revived in 1526, provide
that all *tinajas* must contain two kinds of earth,
one red, the other white, thoroughly compounded
in a trough of water. Before the potter removes
the clay from the trough, he must call the city
supervisor or *veedor* to look into the quality and
mixing of the mass. The vessel as it leaves the
oven must be white ; otherwise, even although it
have no flaw, the inspector is to break it. The
potter is forbidden to coat his *tinajas* with a glaze

XLIX

HISPANO-MORESQUE TAV. 174

composed of eggs, blood, chalk, and other strange
ingredients; nor may he fire the glaze with
torches, "because the smell of the smoke clings
to the *tinaja*, and the wine or stum deposited
therein grows redolent of it, and it stays within
the jar perpetually."

Owing doubtless to their plain, domestic purpose
and their trifling market cost, early *tinajas* are
not often met with. A fine example in excellent
preservation is at South Kensington, and is
described by Riaño as "a wine jar, amphora-
shaped, and ornamented with an incised pattern
of vine leaves, and stamped diaper of a Gothic
character." Several good *tinajas* have been discovered of late years at Seville. Gestoso mentions
six, five of which are glazed. The first of these
was found in 1893, and has a bright green glaze
upon a ground of reddish earth. Both handles
and nearly all the neck are wanting. The decoration consists of various bands or *fajas* round the
body of the jar, a series of archways, another of
leaves, and a central band of stars, three deep,
strongly imprinted from a mould. In every
ninth arch are stamped symbolic hands, such as
we see upon the Gate of Justice of the Alhambra.

The second *tinaja* is similar to the one just

mentioned, except that it has the neck. It was discovered in 1895, and is now in Seville museum.

The third *tinaja* is also in this museum, and was discovered in 1901. It is in a very poor condition, and Gestoso believes that it was originally covered with a honey-coloured glaze.

The fourth *tinaja* was found in a drain, in the same year as the preceding one, and is inscribed with words, including *Blessing* and *Felicity*, in Cufic characters. Gestoso is unable to decide whether this vessel was made at Seville or elsewhere.

The fifth *tinaja* is in the collection of Don José Morón, and possesses greater interest than the others, both because it is in excellent condition, and also because the decoration is entirely in the Spanish-Christian style, without a trace of Saracenic ornament. Small Gothic-looking shields surround the body of this vessel, which is stamped with pomegranates, and with the arms and emblems of the Ponce de León and other families. Between each pair of shields is an oval-shaped medallion containing human figures.

The sixth *tinaja* is unglazed. It was found in June of 1893, and is adorned with repetitions of the words *Prosperity* and *Blessing*, as well as with a series of deer and other animals in the act of running; some of them with birds upon their backs. These designs are very uncommon, and Gestoso has seen no other *tinaja*, proceeding from this region, similarly decorated.

Tinajas are still made in large quantities at Toboso, Lucena, Colmenar de Oreja, and other Spanish towns and villages.

Other large objects of a thoroughly oriental character were earthenware glazed *brocales* or brims of wells, which, like the *tinajas*, were largely manufactured at Seville and Toledo. Specimens of these *brocales* exist in the museums of Toledo and Cordova. Riaño describes one which is at South Kensington. "It was bought at Toledo for three guineas at a shoemaker's shop. It is made of glazed white and green earthenware, with ornamental Cufic characters in high relief all round, which appear to be of the fourteenth century. The inscription, which is repeated, is imperfect, and all that I can decipher are the words 'the power, the excellence, and the peace.'"

Gestoso describes two *brocales* and the fragments of a third. All these objects were found at Seville. The two which are intact, or nearly so, are cylindrical, and of a white ware. One of them has a simple leaf decoration, and seems to have been covered with a green glaze. The other, which was discovered in 1894, is surrounded by a triple band of inscription in African characters which are illegible.

Gestoso also describes some interesting baptismal fonts, a class of object which he pronounces to have been the most important of all that were produced in the potteries of Triana, by reason both of their large dimensions and of their elaborate ornamentation. He states that three methods were employed to decorate these fonts. The first consisted in attaching to their surface small moulded plates which bore the likeness of a saint, flowers, monograms, or other devices. By the second method the decoration was moulded directly on the font; while the third method consisted in a combination of the other two.

Splendid examples of these Spanish fonts exist in various churches of Andalusia and in private collections. One of the finest is in the parish church of Nuestra Señora de la Concepción, at Laguna, Tenerife. It is suggested by Gestoso that this *pila* of Laguna was made at Seville and sent to the Canaries in the year 1479, when orders were issued by Ferdinand and Isabella for the completion of the monasteries in those islands.

Pilas were also manufactured at Toledo, although Gestoso says that the workmanship of those produced at Seville was in every way superior. Nevertheless, he has only found the maker's name upon a single font, which is inscribed with that of Juan Sanchez Vachero, and is now preserved in the church of San Pedro at Carmona. Another remarkable *pila* is that of the hospital of San Lázaro at Seville.

In course of time the Spanish Church forbade the use of *pilas* made of glazed earthenware, and ordered their substitution by fonts of stone or marble. One of these dispositions, included among the *Constituciones Sinodales* of the bishopric of Málaga, and dated 1671, is quoted by Gestoso. It enacts that the *pila* be of stone and not of earthenware, and that if any of this latter class remain, they are to be "consumed" (*i.e.* destroyed) within two months.

Returning to the Ordinances of Granada, those which concern the potters or *olleros* generally are dated 1530, and inform us of the price of glazed and unglazed articles in common use, such as *ollas* or pots (with and without glaze), *cazuelas* or earthen vessels for cooking meat, plates of many colours and dimensions, *jarros* (jugs), *alcuzas* (vials), *cantaros castellanos* (Castilian water-pitchers), *cantaros moriscos* (Moorish water-pitchers [1]), *morteros* (mortars), *lebrillos* (earthen tubs), *candiles* (lamps with a green, white or yellow glaze), *orzas* (gally pots), *botijas* (narrow-necked jars), and *salseras* (saucers).

The shape and colouring of many of these common articles have been continued till to-day, especially in Andalusia. I reproduce a photograph of some (Plate 1.), in which the influence of the East is unmistakable. The smaller of the two unglazed jars is used for carrying and cooling water, and is made at Loja. The other, which is often used for storing honey, is from Guadalajara. The spherical vessel is a kind of bottle for *aguar-*

---

[1] The watersellers' Ordinance of 1516 enacts that each of these vendors shall carry a minimum load of six *cántaros*, and that the *cántaros* themselves shall be "of the round shape, and not the Moorish ones, as these have long spouts ; each *cántaro* to be closed with a cork." The latter is the typical pitcher of Morocco. "As we were talking, neighbours dropped in, in the familiar Eastern way, and sat quiet and self-contained, occasionally drinking from one of the two long-necked and porous water-jars, known as 'Baradas' or the 'coolers,' which stand, their wooden stoppers tied to them with a palmetto cord, on each side the divan."— Cunninghame Graham, *Mogreb-el-Acksa*, p. 88.

L

COARSE SPANISH POTTERY

(*Hudson*)

POTTERY

diente. It is glazed a brightish green, and is made in various parts of Andalusia, as are the gourd-shaped *calabazas,* which have a yellow glaze. The smallest vessel, or that which has a funnel-shaped and bulging mouth, is coated with a coarse metallic glaze coloured in white and blue, and proceeds from Granada.

So is the influence of the Spanish Moors, linking the present intimately to the past, and handed down by early craftsmen to the moderns, and from Mussulmans to Christian Spaniards, maintained and kept alive, not only by the city ordinances I have quoted, but also by the more occult yet no less permanent and cogent force of local and unchronicled tradition. In the historic quarter of Granada which is called the Albaycin, survive a few *alfarerías* to this hour (Plate lxix.). Here, on the potter's wheel or ranged about his yard, may yet be seen the red Granada earth that is believed to have inspired the vase of the Alhambra, applied to-day to common crockery that notwithstanding has a subtle, unfamiliar charm. And towards the time of sundown, when the master turns indoors to supper and his workmen have gone home, when the last of the red light is colouring the ancient city wall until it too looks like a mammoth monument of the potter's art of old Granada, it is a strange experience to wander through these desolate yards, among the files of ruddy Granadino ware kindling with vivid memories of the vanished Mussulmans of Spain, and bringing back to us that spirited old poet of the East who also sang of pottery :—

> "Listen again. One Evening at the Close
> Of Ramazan, ere the better Moon arose,
>   In that old Potter's Shop I stood alone
> With the clay Population round in Rows.
>
> And strange to tell, among that Earthen Lot
> Some could articulate, while others not :
>   And suddenly one more impatient cried—
> 'Who *is* the Potter, pray, and who the Pot?'
>
> Then said another—'Surely not in vain
> My substance from the common Earth was ta'en,
>   That He who subtly wrought me into Shape
> Should stamp me back to common Earth again.'"

MOSAIC-WORK AND TILES

The art of colouring and glazing earthenware was practised by various peoples of the ancient eastern world, and passed, in course of time,

POTTERY

through Egypt to Phœnicia, Greece, and Rome, and, later still, to Mussulman peoples of north-western Africa.

Glazed earthenware was possibly produced in Roman Spain, although the specimens of it which have been discovered are singularly and, indeed, significantly few. Their colour is commonly green or lightish yellow. Gestoso makes particular mention of a small jar now preserved in the museum of Seville, describing it as "of an ordinary shape, but finely made." He admits, however, that no trace of glaze exists in any of the broken Visigothic vessels (copied, as Saint Isidore tells us, from the Roman-Spanish pottery) that were found some years ago among the ruins of Italica. Thus it is not decided whether the Spanish potters learned to glaze, or whether this development of their craft remained familiar to the Spaniards of that period through imported objects merely.

As with glazed earthenware, the origin of mosaic must be looked for in the East. Greece, who had doubtless borrowed it from Egypt, communicated it to Rome at least two centuries before the Christian era, and from this time the Romans used it freely in the decoration of their buildings. The Greek mosaic was composed exclusively of stone. The Romans modified this usage by the introduction of diminutive cubes of clay, painted and baked like porcelain ; and later, in the reign of Claudius, dyed these cubes with various colours.

Roman mosaic-work (commonly in the tessellated style and not the *opus sectile*) has been unearthed in many parts of the Peninsula. Such are the two " mosaics of the Muses," discovered at Italica on December 12th, 1799, and June 12th, 1839 ;[1] other mosaics, to the number of some thirty, discovered from time to time among the same ruins ; another, discovered at Majorca in 1833 ; that of the Calle Batitales at Lugo (the Roman *Lucus Augusti*), discovered in 1842 ; those of Palencia, Gerona, Merida, Milla del Rio (near León), Rielves (near Toledo), Duratón, Aguilafuente, and Paradinas (near Segovia), and Carabanchel, three miles from Madrid. The mosaic found at Lugo is believed to have formed part of a temple dedicated to Diana. The decoration is

---

[1] The latter, which was the finer of the two, was dug out by Don Ivo de la Cortina. It has subsequently been allowed to go to pieces, but a coloured plate depicting it will be found in the first volume of the *Musco Español de Antigüedades*.

POTTERY

partly geometrical, and consists of the head of a man between two dolphins, with other fishes swimming along the border. Laborde describes another mosaic which existed, early in the nineteenth century, in a hall of the archbishop's palace at Valencia. "The pavement of this hall demands particular attention; it is formed of antique pavements, discovered in the month of February, 1777, three hundred paces north-east of the town of Puch, between Valencia and Murviedro; some were entire, others were only fragments. They were separated with care, and placed on the floor of this hall, where they are carefully preserved. They are different mosaics, formed by little stones of three or four lines in diameter, curiously enchased. They are distributed into seven squares in each of which medallions and divers designs have been drawn: their compartments are of blue on a white ground. We observe in one of these squares an imitation of the pavement of Bacchus, discovered at Murviedro, and of which there remained but very few vestiges; it was copied in a drawing-book which a priest of this town had preserved; it is executed with such art and exactness, that no difference can be observed between this modern work and that of the Romans. In

131

another we see Neptune seated in a car, in one hand holding a whip, and in the other a trident and the reins of the horses by which his car is drawn : these appear to be galloping.

" In the same hall are also seen other pavements, of which only fragments could be preserved. Some serve for borders and ornaments to the preceding pavements. On these are represented a tiger, fishes, birds, houses, flowers, and garlands, well executed. There are particularly five stuck on wood and shut up in a closet; on these are birds, fruits, and flowers, figured in different colours, the execution of which is very curious; they are perhaps the most precious of the whole."

The same author says elsewhere : " In digging to make a road from Valencia to Murviedro in 1755, at the entrance of the latter town a mosaic pavement was discovered; it was entire, and of such beauty that it was thought worthy of preservation. Ferdinand the Sixth caused it to be surrounded with walls; but the king's intentions were not properly fulfilled; the gates were suffered to remain open, and every one carried away some part of the pavement, which consequently soon became despoiled; it was rectangular, and measured

132

twenty-four feet by fourteen. There are still some fragments of it in several houses at Murviedro. A priest of that town, Don Diego Puch, an antiquarian, took a drawing of it, which he afterwards had painted at Valencia on the tiles fabricated there, and paved an apartment of his house with them. It was likewise copied with the greatest exactness, with small stones perfectly similar, in an apartment of the library belonging to the archiepiscopal palace, as we have already stated."

Swinburne also mentions a mosaic pavement which he saw at Barcelona, upon the site of what he believed to have been a temple of Neptune. In it were represented "two large green figures of tritons, holding a shell in each hand; between them a sea-horse, and on the sides a serpent and a dolphin."

In October of 1901 a very important and beautiful mosaic was discovered at Italica. It is known as "the mosaic of Bacchus," the worship of which deity, says Señor Quintero, was probably general in Andalusia, owing to her wealth of vines. This mosaic was found at a depth of six feet six inches below the surface of the soil, and measures twenty-one feet square. It is believed to have formed the pavement of a Roman dining-chamber.

Mosaic in the manner of the Greeks and Romans seems in Spain to have disappeared with the Visigoths. That it was known to these is told us by Saint Isidore :—" Pavimenta originem apud graecos habent elaboratae arte picturae, litostrata parvulis crustis ac tesselis tinctis in varios colores." [1]

It is impossible to affirm with any confidence that glazed earthenware, whether in the form of tiles or other objects, was manufactured by the Spanish Moors during the Cordovese Caliphate, or the period of the kinglings of Taifa. No trace of it has been discovered among the scanty ruins of Medina Az-zahará[2] and Az-zahira—ancient

[1] *Tessela* and *crusta* are defined by him as follows : "Tesselae sunt e quibus domicilia sternuntur a tesseris nominata, id est quadratis lapillis, per diminutionem."

" Crustae sunt tabulae marmoris. Unde et marmorari parietes et constati dicuntur. Qui autem marmora secandi in crustas rationem excogitaverunt non constat. Fiunt autem arena et ferro serraque in praetenui linea premente arenas, tractuque ipse secante : sed crassior arena plus erodet marmoris. Nam tenuis fabricis et polituris accomodata est."

[2] Among these ruins, at five miles' distance from the city, pieces of common brick have come to light ; but no glazed pottery of any kind, whether as *foseifesa, azulejos,* or mosaic.

LI

134

DOOR OF THE MIHRAB

(*Showing mosaic-work, Cordova Cathedral*)

POTTERY

palaces of Cordova—or in the marvellous mosque. We know, however, that towards the seventh century the Arabs borrowed from Byzantium the mosaic-work of tessons known as *psephosis fsefysa*, and this, or something similar, was used, though probably to a small extent, among the Muslims of the Spanish Caliphate. Although, towards the middle of the thirteenth century, the historian Aben - Said, a native of Granada, recorded that in Al-Andalus " is made a kind of *mofassass* which is called in the East *alfoseifesa*," remains of this elaborate product only exist to-day at Cordova, where patches may yet be seen lining the dome of the *mirhab* in the vast *aljama* (Plate li.). The mosaic in question is stated to have been a gift from the Byzantine emperor to the sultan Al-Hakem, and was set in place by a skilled workman, a Greek, who, like the offering itself, proceeded from Constantinople.

During his stay at Cordova this Greek was helped by certain of the Sultan's slaves, who thus acquired the secrets of the craft, and practised it thereafter.[1]

Rodrigo Amador de los Rios contends, however,

[1] Dozy's version of *The History of Almagreb*, by Ibn-Adzarí the Moor ; p. 253.

that this decoration is in no sense a true mosaic, but just a tempera painting executed on the wall and overlaid with cubes of glass. In any case, no other specimen of such work has been discovered in any part of the Peninsula.

By the time of the Almohade invasion or very shortly after — that is, towards the twelfth century,—the Spanish Moors had grown acquainted with glazed earthenware. Indeed, the Almohades are believed by some authorities to have actually introduced it. Gestoso, on the contrary, suggests that Spain may have transmitted it to Africa. However this may be, the Almohades used it largely in the decoration of their homes and public buildings in Andalusia; first as *aliceres* or bands composed of smallish pieces running round a room, and subsequently in the more effective and more useful form of *azulejos* proper. The Spanish Moors employed the word *almofassass* to designate both *aliceres* and *azulejos*. Nevertheless, the two were not identical, although Riaño takes them to be so. He says: "The earliest tiles or *azulejos* made in Spain are composed of small pieces let into the wall, forming geometrical patterns." These, in fact, were *aliceres*. It is not so easy to define an *azulejo*. We read in Aben-Said, quoted by

POTTERY

Al-Makkari : " There is another kind of work employed for paving houses. It is called *az-zulechî* and resembles *mofassass*. It has wonderful colouring, and replaces the coloured marble used by the people of the East to decorate their chambers."

This definition is not completely clear. Those of the Christian-Spanish writers are not more satisfactory. Covarrubias calls these objects "small bricks, square and of other shapes, used for lining chambers in the mansions of the wealthy, or in garden paths." Nebrija calls them *tessela pavimenticia*, adding that they bear the name of *azulejos* because the earliest ones were of a blue colour—a statement which Dozy supports by instancing the Persian-Arabic *zaward* or "blue stone."

Gestoso resolves the question sufficiently for our purpose by showing that the term *azulejo* is usually applied to square tiles of a largish size, the length of whose sides varies between eleven centimetres and eighteen centimetres, *aliceres* being properly the smaller strips or pieces (technically known as *cintas* or *verduguillos*) used in a bordering or frieze. Other decorative pieces of small dimensions, invented in the fifteenth

137

century, were called *olambres* or *olambrillas*, and served to lend variety to the red or yellow brick-work of a pavement or a floor.

The production of *azulejos* in Spain may thus be traced to as far back as the twelfth century. By far the most important centre of the craft was Seville. Here, from the twelfth until the fourteenth century, was made the glazed and decorative tiling which consisted of small pieces of monochrome earthenware—black, white, green, blue, or yellow — cut one by one, and pieced together in the manner of a true mosaic. This process, says Gestoso, was lengthy, difficult, and dear. In the fourteenth and fifteenth centuries the same mosaic would often take the form of a series of narrow, white, ribbon-like strips, with coloured interspaces. Specimens of this "ribbon-work tiling" exist to-day in the Patio de Las Doncellas of the Alcázar (Plate lii.). Towards the sixteenth century the Sevillano potters discovered a simpler way of making effective and artistic *azulejos*, which they called the *cuerda seca* process. This novel method consisted in pressing a wood or metal mould upon the unbaked tile, in such a manner that the outline of the pattern remained in slight relief. This outline was next brushed over with

LII

MOSAIC OF THE PATIO DE LAS DONCELLAS

(Alcázar of Seville)

a mixture of manganese and grease, which turns, in baking, very nearly black. The body of the pattern was then filled in with the various colours, which the greasy line completely separated, and thus prepared, the tile was rendered permanent by firing.

This process, in which the patterns are nearly always geometrical, remained in general use until about the year 1550, when it began to be superseded by two others, known respectively as the processes of "cuenca" and "Pisano."

The *cuenca* tile was simple and of excellent effect. The pattern, stamped from a metal mould, remained in bas-relief,—a characteristic which caused these objects to be also known as *azulejos " de relieve."* The shelving border of each hollow stamped into the tile thus formed a kind of natural barrier which kept the colour there deposited from mingling with its neighbours. When of a larger size, and joined in pairs to form between each two a single motive (*ladrillo por tabla*), these *azulejos* were often employed for decorating roofs and ceilings.

The tiles which bear the name of their inventor, Francesco Niculoso Pisano the Italian, who lived and worked for many years at Seville, date from about the same time as the "cuenca" *azulejos*. In the case of the *Pisano* tile, there is no indentation caused by the imprint of a mould, the surface being merely coated with a monochrome glaze, painted upon and fired, the decoration thus remaining flat all over. Commonly the ground is white or yellow, with the colour of the pattern shaded blue, or black, or deepish purple. This process, which lent itself to most elaborate and effective schemes of ornament, remained in vogue until the eighteenth century, and was practised, not only by Pisano himself, but by a long succession of his pupils, followers, and imitators.

Such were the processes in use among the *azulejo*-makers of old Seville. Specimens of their craftsmanship which yet survive and illustrate the various styles and epochs may be thus enumerated :—

(1) Mosaic tile-work, such as appears in Seville at the time of the Almohade invasion. A fragment of this kind of work forms part of the collection of Señor Osma, and proceeds from the church of San Andrés. Tiles and smaller pieces of mosaic-work, coloured in malachite green and white, were also found in 1899 and 1900, in the upper walls of the renowned Torre del Oro, or "Golden

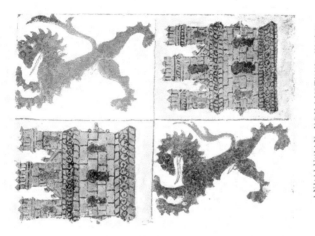

ANDALUSIAN NON-LUSTRED WARE

(A.D. 1350-1406. Osma Collection)

POTTERY

Tower," erected in the year 1220, and which is popularly thought to derive its venerable title from the sparkle of the sun upon its *azulejos*. Another piece of primitive mosaic, measuring rather less than a yard square, and containing star-shaped geometrical devices, was found in 1890 beneath the floor of the cathedral ; while mosaics of a later age, including the more elaborate *lacería* patterns that resemble ribbon, are preserved in the Patio de las Doncellas of the Alcázar, in the Casa de Olea, and in the parish churches of San Estéban, San Gil, and Omnium Sanctorum.

(2) A small group of curious tiles, believed to be anterior to the reign of Pedro the First, has come to light some years ago, in the churches of San Andrés and Santa Marina, and in the Claustro del Lagarto of the cathedral. Those of San Andrés are of white earthenware, glazed in the same colour and stamped from a mould with the figures of two wolves in fairly bold relief (see tailpiece to this chapter). Traces of a glaze of malachite green are on the bodies of these wolves. The *azulejos* of the church of Santa Marina, also discovered recently, are examined by Señor Osma in his pamphlet *Azulejos sevillanos del siglo xiii* (Madrid, 1902). They measure about three and

a half inches square, and bear devices of a castle and an eagle, stamped in the diagonal direction of the tile, showing that this was fixed upon the wall in lozenge fashion. The tiles are bathed upon their surface with what is termed by Osma "the semi-transparent, caramel-coloured glaze peculiar to the pottery of Moorish Spain."[1] Upon this ground is stamped the decoration,—the eagles in the blackish purple of baked manganese, the castles without additional colour, so as to be distinguished only by their outline from the yellowish surface of the tile.

The *azulejos* of the Claustro del Lagarto of the cathedral are three in number, and were found in 1888. Two of them are stamped with a castle of a single tower described within a shield, and the third with a Greek cross. These are considered by Osma to be the only tiles existing at this moment which date from the latter third of the thirteenth century. In fact, he places their manufacture between the years 1252 and 1269.

(3) *Cuerda seca* tiles. Handsome *zocalos* or dadoes of these tiles are in the Casa de los

---

[1] According to Gestoso, the colours in use among the Almohades consisted of green, black, caramel or honey, and deep purple. These colours underwent no change until the sixteenth century.

LIV

142

CUENCA TILES

(Alcázar of Sevilla)

POTTERY

Pinelos, and in the chapels of the palaces of the Dukes of Alba and Medinaceli. Gestoso attributes them to the end of the fifteenth century or the beginning of the sixteenth. Detached *cuerda seca* tiles are preserved in the municipal museum of archæology, while a fine pair (Plate liii.) of this class of *azulejos* belongs to Señor Osma, who considers they were made between 1480 and 1495. They are thus coeval with the no less interesting dish of the time of Ferdinand and Isabella, of which a reproduction is given opposite page 190.

(4) *Cuenca* tiles. Quantities of these, dating from the sixteenth and seventeenth centuries, may yet be seen in many parts of Seville ; for instance, in her churches or her convents, in her superb Alcázar, or in the mansions of her old nobility. Probably the most remarkable of all are those in the gardens of the Alcázar, and lining the walls of the Pavilion of Charles the Fifth. The devices on these polychrome *azulejos* (16th century ; Plate liv.) are very numerous, including men and animals, centaurs and other monsters, the Pillars of Hercules, and imitations of elaborate dress fabrics.

(5) *Pisano* tiles. Although some facts have been unearthed concerning the Italian Francesco Niculoso Pisano, we do not know pre-

cisely in what year he came to Seville, or in what year he died. Davillier thought it probable that he had studied at Faenza or at Caffagiolo. At all events, it was Pisano who broadly launched the art of the Sevillian potters on the stream of the Renaissance.[1] I have stated that the tiles which bear his name are painted on a white or yellow ground. Consequently their surface is flat, without the ridges and depressions of the *cuenca* or the *cuerda seca* methods. We find *Pisano* tiles applied to various objects, such as tombs, altars, friezes, and archivolts. This artist, says Gestoso, further introduced the use of two new colours,— violet and rose. Several of his best productions are still intact, including the doorway of the church of the monastery of Santa Paula (in which he was assisted by a Spanish master, Pedro Millan), and the altar of the Catholic Sovereigns in the Alcázar. Both these masterpieces were executed in the year 1504, and bear Pisano's signature. The doorway of Santa Paula is described by Gestoso as consisting of a single body of masonry, distinct from that of the building itself, though

---

[1] Gestoso says that florid Gothic and Renaissance motives are found occasionally in the older *cuenca* tiles. This was, however, quite exceptional.

resting against it, and constructed of bricks of
uniform size, which show us, by their perfect
symmetry, how skilful were the masons of that
time, with whom the Moorish craftsmanship was
yet a living power. The doorway is formed by a
series of concentric Gothic arches resting on
slender pillars. The space which forms the outer
archivolt is most remarkable. Upon a ground
of *azulejos* which copy the colour of the brickwork,
we see a number of Plateresque designs of exquisite beauty, painted in white and blue, with
occasional touches of other colours. Among
the devices are chimeras, war-trophies, volutes,
chaplets, parapegms, antelopes, masks, and others
which are characteristic of the Florentine Renaissance. Upon this ground, and enclosed by circular
garlands in high relief, consisting of polychrome
fruits and flowers, are seven medallions containing
figures of male and female saints, except the one
which is upon the keystone, and which represents
the birth of Christ. In this medallion the figures
are enamelled in white upon a cobalt-blue ground,
recalling, as also do the garlands, the work of the
celebrated della Robbia.[1] In the rest of the

[1] A plaque belongs to Señor Gestoso which proceeds from the
demolished Mudejar church of San Miguel at Seville. It measures

medallions the figures are glazed in brilliant colours. In the three medallions upon the left, beginning with the lowest one, we see, upon the first, Saint Helen ; upon the second, two saints in monkish dress ; and upon the third, Saint Peter and Saint Paul. On the medallions of the other side are another saint dressed as a monk, San Cosmé, San Damián, and San Roque. The spaces on either side of the archivolt are covered with tiles which represent a landscape. In each of the upper angles is an angel holding a large tablet with IHS in ornamental Gothic character upon a black ground. These letters, and also the angels and the frames of the tablets, are enamelled in gold. Beneath each tablet is an angel standing with extended wings upon a bracket of lustred earthenware, and holding an open book. The brickwork of the door is closed

fifteen inches high by ten wide, and is decorated with a representation, in bas-relief, of the Coronation of the Virgin. The eyebrows, eyelids, and lips of the figures are executed in cobalt upon a thick layer of white glaze, and strongly recall the method of Lucca della Robbia. Gestoso considers that this plaque was made in the latter part of the fourteenth century. If so, it is antecedent to the work of della Robbia (whose *Resurrection* upon one of the doors of the Duomo of Florence dates from 1438) by a good many years. A similar example, also by an unknown hand and representing the Coronation, is in the chapel of the Sagrario of Seville Cathedral.

146

POTTERY

by a plain impost supporting a small battlement
covered with *cuenca* tiles, and crowned with a
cornice of flamboyant ornaments alternating with
the heads of cherubs glazed in white, and with a
white marble cross in the centre. The tympanum
is embellished by a superb shield carved in high
relief upon white marble with the arms of Castile,
León, Aragon, and Sicily, surmounted by a royal
crown and the eagle with the nimbus. Beside this
shield are two smaller ones of *azulejos* painted with
the yoke and sheaf of arrows, and the motto TĀTO
MŌTA. The ground on which are executed these
three shields occupies the whole tympanum, and
is covered with Plateresque devices including two
tablets, on one of which we read the letters S.P.Q.R.,
and on the other, PISANO. Above the first of these
tablets is another of an oval shape, bearing the word
NICULOSO. Lastly, at the base of the archivolt,
and on the left-hand side of the spectator, is a very
small rectangular tablet with this inscription :—

NICVLOSO

FRANCISCO–I–

TALIANO–MEF

ECIT INELAGNO DEI

· 154 ·

The altar in the Alcázar of the same city, and which is known as that of the Catholic Sovereigns (Plate lv.), is entirely covered with "Pisano" *azulejos* measuring sixteen centimetres square. Imbedded in the centre is a picture, also of painted tiles, representing the visit of the Virgin to Saint Elizabeth. This picture measures five feet in height by three feet eight inches in breadth. Beneath it is the figure of a patriarch resting his head upon his hand. Boughs with large flowers issue from his breast, and among the flowers are half-length figures of the prophets, together with those of Jesus and the Virgin, the whole of this decoration forming a frame to the central picture. The rest of the altar is profusely decorated with designs in the Renaissance style, consisting of vases, animals, genii, and the emblems of Ferdinand and Isabella. In the centre of the tiling which forms the altar-front is a circular picture made of *azulejos* surrounded by a garland of fruits and laurel leaves, and representing the Annunciation, garland and picture being supported by two monsters with the tails of dragons and the upper parts of women. Large flaming torches rest between the outstretched arms of the monsters, and round about or springing from them are flowers, animals,

LV

ALTAR OF THE CATHOLIC SOVEREIGNS

POTTERY

cornucopias, and other decoration. The entire
retablo is painted lightish blue and white upon a
yellow ground, except the larger picture and its
decorative border, which is of a deeper blue. A
small tablet beneath the Virgin's feet contains the
words NICULOSO FRANCESCO ITALIANO ME FECIT, and
on the pilaster represented on the left hand of the
same picture is added the date, 1504. As Gestoso,
Davillier, and others have remarked, it is evident
that while the rest of the altar is pure Renaissance-
Plateresque, the pictures copied on the tiles are of
a northern school. Probably they were designed
for Niculoso by one of the various German or
Flemish masters who at that time were resident
in Seville.

Another altar which was formerly in the same
palace, but which has disappeared, was also
painted by this craftsman. It was described by
Cean Bermudez as containing scenes from the
life of the Virgin, the Trinity, and the two Saints
John, and bore the same date as the altar which
is yet existing, namely, 1504.

Among the other works of Niculoso are the
altar of the church of Tentudia, the tomb of
Iñigo Lopez in the church of Santa Ana in the
quarter of Triana, and a tile-picture representing,

similarly to the one which forms the centre of the altar in the Alcázar, the Virgin's visit to Saint Elizabeth. This picture formerly belonged to the kings of Portugal, and is now in the museum of Amsterdam.[1]

Such were the decorative *azulejos* which made the potteries of Seville famous throughout Europe, and which are known to have been exported to Italy, Portugal, and even England.[2] The names of several hundred mediæval and post-mediæval makers of these Seville tiles have been exhumed and published by Gestoso.

The general title of the Spanish potter was *ollero*, a comprehensive term which reaches from the most ambitious *azulejero* to the maker of the

---

[1] Certain *azulejos*, signed by Niculoso and dated 1500, were formerly existing in the palace of the Counts of El Real de Valencia in the city of this name. These tiles were executed in relief, and proved that Niculoso did not work exclusively in the Italian style.

[2] In Portugal, tiles which Gestoso believes to have been made at Seville, exist in Coimbra cathedral, the church of San Roque at Lisbon, and the two palaces of Cintra. In our own country, Seville tiles are stated by Marryat and Demmin to line the walls of the Mayor's Chapel at Bristol, whither they were doubtless conveyed by one of the numerous English merchants who traded between Spain and England, and who are known to have made their home at Seville in the sixteenth century. Another tile of Seville workmanship, proceeding from Haccombe Church, Devonshire, is in the British Museum.

meanest kitchen-ware. The *olleros* of older
Seville produced for centuries, not only glazed
and coloured tiling by the processes already
indicated, but countless other objects such as
brims of wells, apothecary's jars, baptismal fonts,
and dishes of every shape and size. They used a
general mark (the tower of the Giralda) to stamp
their pottery; but private marks are nearly
always absent. The facts that have appeared in
recent years concerning these artificers are seldom
interesting. The mere mention of a name is
meaningless, or even perplexing, seeing that a
Moor or Mudejar would frequently assume the
name and surname of a Christian. Nevertheless,
Gestoso has brought to light important notices
concerning one or two, and in particular a document dating from the reign of Ferdinand and
Isabella, relating to a celebrated potter of that
period named Fernan Martinez Guijarro. This
document, which is dated 1479, describes Martinez
as "a very great master in the art of making
azulejos, fonts, and all the things pertaining to
his trade, insomuch that none other in all this
kingdom is like unto him," and subsequently,
"considering him to be so excellent a craftsman
that persons come hither from Portugal and other

parts to purchase and to carry off his ware." It is further stated that Martinez Guijarro was in wealthy circumstances ("hombre rrico e de mucha rrenta e fasyenda"). His *talleres* or workshops were in the *barrio* of Triana, and included (as we learn from one of the documents copied by the same investigator) a separate department for the manufacture or storage of lustred ware.

Unfortunately, even Gestoso is unable to point to any piece of tiling or other pottery now existing, as being unquestionably executed by this master.

Another Sevillian potter of exceptional merit was Cristóbal de Augusta, who worked in the latter half of the sixteenth century, and left his name upon the *azulejo* dadoes of the Halls of Charles the Fifth in the Alcázar. The style of these most brilliant tiles is pure Renaissance, and forms a worthy continuation of the splendid work of Niculoso. Augusta, indeed, is termed in the Archives of the Alcázar "master of making tiles in the Pisano manner" (*del pisano*).[1] Some tile-makers of little note succeeded him, but even the names of these are carefully recorded by Gestoso.

[1] The *pisano* process is believed by Gestoso to have succumbed before the *cuenca*. He says he is aware of no *pisano* tiling which can be dated from as late as the second half of the seventeenth century.

POTTERY

Seville was thus the principal centre of the craft of decorative tile-making. *Azulejos* were also made at Barcelona and other towns in Cataluña, at Talavera de la Reina, Burgos, Toledo, Granada, and Valencia, in several towns of Aragon, and probably at Cordova. Riaño quotes a letter written about the year 1422, from the wife of the Admiral of Castile to the abbess of the nunnery of Santo Domingo at Toledo, requesting that a number of *azulejos* be sent to her. "She alludes, in the same letter, to painted tiles, and says she was expecting a master potter from Seville to place the tiles in their proper places. This shows us" (continues Riaño) "that it was only in the province of Andalusia that the art was known of cutting these tiles into geometrical sections and mosaic patterns."

The meaning of this passage is obscure. Riaño speaks of painted tiles and *azulejos* as though they were distinct objects, and yet they are essentially the same. Again, if only Andalusia was able to produce such tiles, why did the Almirante's wife order them from Toledo? Perhaps the faulty English of Riaño's handbook is responsible, but, as it stands, this passage tells us practically nothing. In any case, abundant evidence exists to show that large quantities of Mudejar and Renaissance tiles were manufactured at Toledo. In general appearance, they are similar to those of Seville.

Ramírez de Arellano believes that decorative tiles were manufactured at Cordova in the fourteenth and fifteenth centuries, and quotes, in proof of this, the names of " maestros de hacer vidriado " or makers of glazed ware, who resided at this ancient capital. One of these craftsmen was Alonso Rodriguez the younger, who, on June 7th, 1574, sold to a canon of the cathedral ten thousand white and green tiles of a common kind (*ladrillos*), probably employed for roofing. The price was three ducats the thousand. On April 10th, 1598, Juan Sanchez engaged to supply the same temple with the same quantity of glazed tiles (*tejas*) for roofing, coloured white, green, and yellow, at sixteen *maravedis* each tile.

Azulejos were certainly made at Granada in the sixteenth and seventeenth centuries, and probably earlier.

In a passage of the Alhambra palace leading from the Patio de la Alberca to the Cuarto Dorado, a space was laid bare not many years ago, containing the original *mostagueras* or small tiles used for flooring, glazed in two colours ; and in the

LVI

THE GATE OF WINE
(Showing polychrome tiling, Alhambra, Granada)

POTTERY

same building, although in constantly diminishing quantities, are large numbers of tiles which date from the time of the Spanish Moors. There has been a good deal of discussion as to whether the roofs of the Alhambra were originally covered with decorative tiles. Swinburne (who must not, however, be taken as the safest of authorities) wrote that "in Moorish times the building was covered with large painted and glazed tiles, of which some few are yet to be seen."

Indifferent Renaissance tiles, made in the reign of Philip the Fifth, are still preserved in parts of the Alhambra.

Excellent polychrome *cuerda seca* tiles (fourteenth century), in white, green, yellow, blue, and black, are over the horseshoe archway of the Gate of Wine of the Alhambra (Plate lvi.). According to Gómez Moreno,[1] they were manufactured here, as were the Moorish *azulejos*, yellow, black, white, violet, and sky-blue, in the Mirador de Daraxa.[2]

[1] *Guía de Granada* ; pp. 35, 36.
[2] Pure red is the rarest of the colours employed in Moorish tile-work. It is, however, found in a single part of the Alhambra ; namely, among the superb tile-decoration of the Torre de la Cautiva.

Gestoso says that red was practically unknown among the Seville potters. Sometimes, however, in coats of arms, a space that

ARTS AND CRAFTS OF OLDER SPAIN

The archives of the Moorish palace also state that towards the close of the sixteenth century Antonio Tenorio, whose pottery was situated in the Secano, and consequently within a stone's-throw of the Casa Real, made several sets of *azulejos* for the Hall of the Abencerrajes. Good Morisco tiles, dating from the same period and wrought by craftsmen such as Gaspar Hernandez, Pedro Tenorio, and the members of the Robles family, are in the Sala de Comares, and in one of the rooms of the Casa de los Tiros.

From the thirteenth century until the eighteenth, excellent *azulejos* were made in Cataluña. Specimens of every period exist in the collections of Don Francisco Rogent and Don José Font y Gumá, of Barcelona, and Don Luis Santacana, of Martorell. The tiles belonging to these gentlemen proceed from the cathedral and other temples of Barcelona, and from the monasteries or castles of Poblet, Santas Creus, Montserrat, Marmellá, San Miguel de Ervol, Centellas, Torre Pallaresa, San Miguel del Fay, and Vallpellach.[1]

should have properly been gules was left uncoloured in the actual making of the tile, and painted red with oil-colour after firing.

[1] Coloured plates of Catalan and other Spanish *azulejos* are published with García Llansó's text in the *Historia General del Arte* : Vol. II.

POTTERY

Another region which has long been celebrated for its *azulejeria* is the kingdom of Valencia. Even in the eighteenth century, when this craft was generally in a state of great decadence, Valencian tiles were thoroughly well made, although the patterns on them were defective. Laborde pronounced them "the best executed and most elegant in Europe," and further said of this locality; "the painted earthenware tiles or *azulejos* are used in the country, but only a small part of them; a great many are sent into the interior of Spain as well as to Cadiz, where they are shipped for Spanish America, and to Marseilles, whence they are conveyed into Africa."

The same writer inserts an interesting account of the manufacture of these *azulejos*. "It is at Valencia that the tiles of earthenware are made, with which they incrust walls and pave apartments : those tiles are of a clayey earth, which is found in the territories of Quarte near Valencia; they harden the earth long after soaking it in water; the tiles are formed in moulds, and are dried in the sun ; they are then beaten with a piece of square wood of the dimensions of which they are wanted. They are then put into the oven, where they undergo a slight baking. As soon as they are done they are glazed, and are afterwards painted in water colours with whatever subject is intended to be represented. The tiles are then replaced in the oven so as not to touch one another, and that the action of the fire may penetrate them all equally : as the colours change by baking, the workmen apply them anew in proportion to the changes that take place ; the red alone alters entirely. The varnish with which they are glazed is made with lead, tin, and white sand. These three substances are ground in a mill to powder, which is mixed with water, to form a paste, and baked in the oven; it is again pounded and put into the oven, where it crystallises : being once more reduced to powder and diluted with water, it becomes varnish. There are two kinds of it ; one is whiter than the other, though the same materials are used : the mode of mixing alone makes the difference ; the whiter, the clearer the tiles. It takes a certain number of tiles to form a picture : they are of different dimensions ; the smallest are three inches nine lines, the largest seven inches nine lines. The price varies according to the size of the tile, the beauty of the varnish, and the variety of the drawings : the lowest price is eight pesos

LVII

TILES OF THE DECADENT PERIOD

POTTERY

(25s.) a thousand, and the highest 100 pesos or £15, 12s. 6d. There is a considerable demand for them; they are superior both in beauty and strength to those used in Holland."

Bourgoing, author of the *Nouveau Voyage en Espagne*, described, in 1789, the same product in the following terms: "L'industrie des Valenciens tire d'ailleurs parti de toutes les productions de leur sol. Il contient une espèce de terre dont ils font ces carreaux de faïence colorée, connus sous le nom d'*Azulejos*, et qu'on ne fabrique qu'à Valence. On en pave les appartements, et on en revêt leurs lambris; on y peint les sujets les plus compliqúes, tels par exemple qu'un bal masqúe, une fête de taureaux. La couleur rouge est la seule qui ne puisse être fixée sur cette espèce de faïence; elle s'altere entièrement par la cuisson."[1]

For the amusement of my readers, I insert an illustration of common Spanish tiles of the decadent period (Plate lvii.), displaying considerable liveliness combined with reckless ignorance of draughtsmanship. A class of these degenerate tiles, made in large quantities at Seville in the eighteenth century, is known as *azulejos de montería* or "hunting-tiles," since episodes of the

Vol. iii., p. 56.

chase form one of the favourite themes of their design.

Although it passed through a long period of prostration, embracing the greater part of the seventeenth and eighteenth centuries, at no time has the manufacture of decorative Spanish tiles succumbed completely. Of recent years it has revived surprisingly at Seville, Barcelona, and Segovia; and at the first of these cities the older *azulejos*, and particularly those in the *cuenca* style, are imitated to perfection.

In the cheapest kinds of modern tiling, such as is used for corridors and kitchens, a common device is a series of repeated curves and dots which evidently has its source in Arabic lettering. Indeed, the ornamental and attractive written characters of the Spanish Moors, rendered familiar to their rivals through long centuries of intercourse, seem to have constantly found favour with the Christian Spaniards. The *fuero* of Jaca, dated A.D. 1064, tells us that a Christian prince of Spain, Don Sancho Ramirez, was accustomed to write his signature in Arabic lettering. Meaningless inscriptions in the same language, and evidently executed by a Christian hand, are engraved on objects in the Royal Armoury; and Señor Osma

POTTERY

describes in an interesting pamphlet (*Los letreros ornamentales en la cerámica morisca del Siglo XV.*) how, in the pottery of older Spain, a word in Arabic such as *alafia* ("prosperity" or "blessing") would often be corrupted by Morisco craftsmen into a motive of a purely ornamental character, and which would only in this sense be comprehended and appreciated by the Christian.[1]

HISPANO-MORESQUE LUSTRED POTTERY

Probably no pottery in the world possesses greater loveliness or interest than the celebrated, yet even to this day mysterious, lustred ware of Moorish Spain.   Our knowledge of the early history of this ware is still imperfect.   In modern

---

[1] *Alafia* is written in Neshki, الْعَافِيَة , which word, says

Señor Osma, by suppressing the diacritical points and prolonging some of the lines, was converted by the potter into the conventional and exclusively decorative device :—

times, attention was first drawn to the lustre process by M. Riocreux, of the Sèvres Museum. In spite, however, of the subsequent monographs and researches of Davillier and other authorities, the origin of lustred pottery is yet a problem which awaits solution. Until some years ago it was believed to have had its source in Persia, where many specimens have been discovered in the form of tiles and other objects; but this belief was afterwards shaken by Fouquet, who unearthed at Fostat in Egypt, in the year 1884, specimens of lustred ware which are known to date from the eleventh century. Saladin, too, affirms that he has seen upon the mosque of Kairuan lustred plaques with inscriptions recording them to have been presented, between A.D. 864 and 875, by the emir Ibrahim Ahmed-ibn-el-Aglab.

Whatever these facts may signify, it appears from a statement by the geographer Edrisi that lustred ware was made in Spain as early as the twelfth century. "Here," said the writer, speaking of Calatayud, "is produced the gold-coloured pottery which is exported to all countries." The next allusion to it is by the traveller Ibn-Batutah, who visited certain parts of Spain in the middle of the fourteenth century. "At Málaga," he

POTTERY

wrote, "is made the beautiful golden pottery which is exported to the farthest countries." These passages refer respectively to Aragon and Andalusia. The same ware was produced in Murcia. Ibn-Said, quoted by Al-Makkari, mentions the "glazed and gilded porcelain" of Murcia, Málaga, and Almería, calling it "strange and admirable." It was also manufactured, probably in larger quantities than in any other part of Spain, in many towns and villages of the kingdom of Valencia, such as Carcer, Alaquaz, Moncada, Quarte, Villalonga, Traiguera, and Manises. In the *Excellencies of the Kingdom of Valencia*, written by Eximenes and published in 1499, we find it stated that "surpassing everything else is the ware of Manises, gilded and painted with such mastery that all the world is enamoured thereof, insomuch that the pope, the cardinals, and princes send for it, astonished that objects of such excellence can be made of earth."[1]

Other writers on the same locality, such as Diago and Escolano, author of the *Historia de la insigne*

[1] "*Sobre tot es la bellessa de la obra de manizes daurada é maestriuolment pintada que ja tot lo mon ha enamorat entàt que lo papa, é los cardenals é lo princeps del mon per special gracia la requeren é stan marauellats que d'terra se puxa fer obra axi excellent é noble.*"

163

y coronada ciudad y reino de Valencia (Valencia, 1610, 1611), confirm this eulogy of Eximenes. According to Escolano, Valencian ware was "of such loveliness that in return for that which the Italians send us from Pisa, we send them boatloads of it from Manises." One of the most recent of authorities on lustred ware remarks that "in the fifteenth century ornamental vases in the (Spanish-Moorish) wares appear to have been commanded from Spain by wealthy Florentines, as is evident from the Medici arms and impresa in fig. 40; others bearing the Florentine lily (fig. 41) seem to have been ordered from the same city." The illustrations to which the author of this monograph[1] refers, depict a vase and a boccale, both in lustred ware, and which it is extremely probable were manufactured at Manises.

The same ware was also possibly made in Cataluña, where pieces of it have been found among the ruins of the village of Las Casas. *La Alhambra*, a small magazine which is published at Granada, contains, in the number dated September 30th, 1901, an account of these fragments by their finder, Joaquín Vilaplana.

[1] Wallis, *The Oriental Influence on Italian Ceramic Art.* London : 1900.

POTTERY

Some years ago the Balearic Islands were also thought to have produced this pottery. One of the earliest and most fervent champions of this theory, now definitely shown to be erroneous, was Baron Davillier. This gentleman, in some respects an excellent authority on Spanish cera- mics, relied too strongly on certain assurances made him by a Señor Bover, and ended by declar- ing that in the museums of Paris and London he had himself seen lustred plates which bore the arms of Ynca in the Balearics, proving them to have been manufactured at that town.

However, a Majorcan archæologist, named Al- varo Campaner, refuted one by one Davillier's points of argument, and showed beyond all question that both the plates of Ynca and the arms which decorated them were simply non- existent, and that the term *Majolica*, deriving from *Majorica*, applies to pottery in general, and not with any preference to lustred ware. Campaner also suggested very ingeniously that the word *Majolica* was probably applied by the Italians to Catalan or Valencian pottery conveyed to Italy in vessels themselves belonging to the Balearics, and which were in the habit of com- pleting their cargoes in the ports of Barcelona and Valencia, and he added that this suggestion is supported by the fact that specimens of lustred ware are far more often met with on the Balearic coast than in the towns and villages of the interior. It is only fair to state that Davillier frankly and fully recognized the value of Campaner's refutation.

As to the methods of producing lustred pottery, the chemical investigations practised by Riocreux, Brogniart, Carand, and others, have shown that the metals used to produce the characteristic reflex which gives the ware its name were copper and silver, entering into the composition of an extremely thin glaze extended over the surface of the pottery, and employed, sometimes together, and sometimes separately. It is obvious that the lustre produced by copper would be deeper, redder, and less delicate than that produced by silver, while varying gradations would be obtainable by the mixture of both metals. It is also beyond doubt that the oldest specimens of this pottery extant to-day are those which contain the palest and most pearly lustre, and consequently the largest quantity of the costlier metal. In those of later date there is an evident inferiority, both in colour, lustre, and design. In fact, two separate, or nearly separate, epochs of this

POTTERY

branch of Spanish pottery are pointed out by
Señor Mélida, who gives the name of *Mudejar*
to lustred objects manufactured at an earlier time
by Moorish artists working in the cities captured
by the Christians, and that of *Morisco* to the
second or inferior class produced by Morisco
craftsmen after the reconquest, and distinguished
by the coarser and degenerate lustre, colouring,
and draughtsmanship.

The rarest and most beautiful examples of this
ware are naturally those which belong to the
former class, and consist of various kinds of plates
and other objects in which elaborate devices such
as lions, antelopes, and shields of heraldry, often
combined with foliage and inscriptions in Gothic
lettering, are coloured in bistre or pale blue,[1] and
rendered doubly beautiful by the delicate nacreous
lustre.

In nearly every case it is extremely difficult to
determine with any certainty the date of manufacture of these objects, as well as the locality.
Wallis says he is aware of "no example of Spanish
lustre pottery antecedent to those in the class to

---

[1] In lustred pottery these colours, and particularly blue, are far
the commonest. It has been found that other colours, such as
green and black, were ill adapted to the lustre process.

which the large Palermo jar belongs, and they are not likely to be much earlier than the end of the fourteenth century. Happily the celebrated plaque (Plate lviii.) formerly belonging to Fortuny, and now in the possession of Excmo Sr. Don G. J. de Osma, furnishes an early date, which, according to its owner, is between May 1408 and November 1417. Those who know the original will remember that it is no less remarkable for the quality of its golden lustre than for the grace and elegance of its fanciful Oriental design." It is also believed by Señor Osma that this plaque was manufactured in the kingdom of Granada; *i.e.* either at Granada or Málaga.

A specimen of Spanish lustred ware more celebrated even than Fortuny's plaque is the "vase of the Alhambra" (Plate lix.), which rests to-day in a corner of the Sala de las Dos Hermanas. The history of this mighty jar is interesting. Popular superstition affirms it to have been discovered, filled to the brim with gold, by the Marquis of Mondejar, first of the Christian governors of the fortress of Granada. Exposed for many years to every stress of weather and to every mutilation at the hands of passersby, it stood, in company with other vases of

168

LVIII

HISPANO-MORESQUE LUSTRED PLAQUE

(Early 15th Century. Oમાં Collection)

enormous size, upon a rampart which is now the
garden terrace known as the Adarves. Several
of the older travellers have described these vessels
or alluded to them. Marmol wrote of them as
far back as the sixteenth century, while the
journal of Bertant de Rouen contains the following
notice ;—"Sur la première terrasse par où l'on
entre, et d'où l'on a de la peine à regarder en
bas sans estre éblöuy, il y a deux fontaines jaillis-
santes, et tout du long des murs du chasteau, des
espaliers d'orangers et de grenadiers, avec de
grands vases de terre peinte, aussi belle que la
porcelaine, où il n'y avoit pour lors, sinon quelques
fleurs en quelques-uns : mais où l'on dit que le
Marquis de Mondejar trouva quantité d'or que les
Mores avaient caché dans la terre, quand il y fût
estably par Ferdinand." The priest Echeverría,
who forged the relics of the ancient Alcazaba of
Granada,[1] was careful to repeat this fable in the
twenty-sixth chapter of his *Paseos por Granada*.
The first edition of this work was published in
1764, under the assumed name of Joseph Romero
Yranzo. There were then two vases and part of
a third, all "lacerated, peeled, and maltreated."

[1] I have fully described these forgeries in Chapters II and III of
Granada : Memories, Adventures, Studies, and Impressions.

169

ARTS AND CRAFTS OF OLDER SPAIN

The Englishman Swinburne wrote in 1776 that below the Towers of the Bell, "on the south-side, on a slip of terrace, is the governor's garden, a very pleasant walk, full of fine orange and cypress trees and myrtle hedges, but quite abandoned. The view it commands is incomparable. Two large vases enamelled with gold and azure foliages and characters are the only ornaments left : these were taken out of the vaults under the royal apartments." In the second edition of Echeverría's *Paseos*, which was republished in 1814, it is added in a footnote that only a single vase remained, "in a room that overlooks the Court of Myrtles." Lozano, however, in his *Antigüedades Arabes*, mentions two vases as existing at the same period. Argote de Molina (*Nuevos Paseos por Granada*, published about 1808) describes, together with the wretchedly executed marble statues in the Sala de las Ninfas, the "two or three great porcelain jars whereof some pieces only now remain," and reminds us that according to the old tradition these statues looked continually towards the vases, which were full of treasure. Argote, nevertheless, takes Echeverría sharply to task for his absurdities upon this theme; and Washington Irving, a diligent gleaner in Eche-

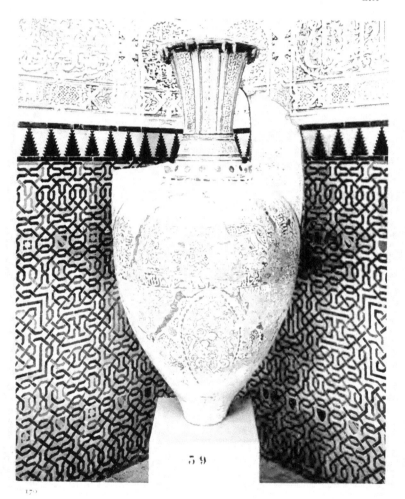

LIX

HISPANO-MORESQUE LUSTRED VASE

(Alhambra, Granada)

POTTERY

verría's somewhat scanty field, makes use of the same material for his well-known story.

In the time of Owen Jones the one surviving vase, now standing with a wooden rail before it in a corner of the Hall of the Two Sisters, still occupied the "room that looks upon the Court of Myrtles." Jones wrote of it in 1842 :—"This beautiful vase was discovered, it is said, full of gold in one of the subterranean chambers of the Casa Real. It is at present to be seen in a small chamber of the Court of the Fish-pond, in which are deposited the archives of the palace. It is engraved in the Spanish work by Lozano, *Antigüedades Arabes de España*, with another of the same size, which was broken a few years ago, and the pieces sold to a passing traveller. The vase is executed in baked clay, with enamelled colours and gold similar to the mosaics."

A more precise description is the following. The vase, which measures four feet six inches in height by eight feet two inches and a half in circumference, is of common earthenware painted with intricate devices fired after painting. This was a difficult operation in a vessel of such size ; and here, in consequence, the colours have slightly run and mingled. Besides these technical flaws, the belly of the vase is broken clean in half, and one of the handles is missing. The shape is amphoraic, with a moderate downward curve. About the middle, surrounded by leaf and stem and geometrical devices effectively intertwined, are two antelopes. The vase is coloured blue and caramel upon a delicate yellow ground, and has a faint metallic lustre.[1] An Arabic inscription is repeated several times, and consists of the words " Felicity " and " Welcome."

This vase is believed to date from the fourteenth century ; and if we judge from the colour and composition of the earth employed, it appears probable that it was made at Granada. Together with the other vases which have disappeared,[2] it was doubtless meant to serve as a receptacle for water, and for decorating the chambers of the palace, where it would rest in amphora-fashion on a perforated stand, while smaller vases containing flowers would fill the niches which may

[1] This lustre is faint but quite distinguishable, and Rada y Delgado was clearly in error in supposing that there is none.

[2] The lost jar mentioned by Owen Jones, of which a drawing has been made, was of the same shape as the one which now remains ; but in its decoration were included the arms of the Nasrite dynasty of Granada. It is this circumstance which has induced Gómez Moreno to suppose that these vases were the work of Granadino artists.

LX

HISPANO-MORESQUE LUSTRED VASE.
(Madrid Museum)

yet be seen in various inner walls of the Alhambra. The belief of Argote[1] and many other writers that these niches were intended to receive the slippers of the Moors is utterly unfounded.

Until quite recently all published illustrations of the great *jarrón de la Alhambra* were inaccurate, and as a rule grotesquely so. Among the very worst are those inserted in the handbooks of Riaño and Contreras. I am glad to be able to reproduce an excellent photograph, which both corrects the atrocious cuts I have observed elsewhere, and relieves me from giving a prolix and possibly a wearisome description of the decoration on the vase.

Several other lustred vases of large size are still preserved in Spain and other countries. One, proceeding from a Sicilian church, is in the museum of Palermo. Wallis, who inserts an illustration, describes it as "amphora-shaped, with two large flat handles ; pear-shaped body, long neck, ribbed at lower part, canellated above, moulded lip. Whitish body, tin glaze. Ornament painted in gold lustre on white ground, the pattern in parts almost obliterated. Hispano-

---

[1] "*Los nichos para chinelas,*" as he calls them, in describing the Sala de Comares.

Moresque. Height, one metre, seventeen centimetres."

Another of these great vases belonged to the painter Fortuny, and was sold at his death to Prince Basilewsky, for thirty thousand francs. It was found by Fortuny at the village of Salar, near Granada, and purchased by him at a low price. "The neck and mouth resemble those of the Alhambra vase. The ornamentation is distributed about the body of the vase in four zones ; one of the two central zones has tangent circles, and the other an inscription."

Another large lustred vase is in the museum of Madrid (Plate lx.). It was found by a labourer at Hornos in the province of Jaen, and passed into the hands of the village priest, who placed it in his church to support the font of holy water. In course of time a dealer in antiquities, by name Amat, happened to pass that way, observed the vase, and made an offer for it to the *padre*. This latter at first refused, but subsequently, stimulated by an ignorant though well-intentioned and disinterested zeal for bettering the temple, he stipulated that if the dealer provided a new support of marble for the font, and paid for white washing the church, he might bear off the coveted

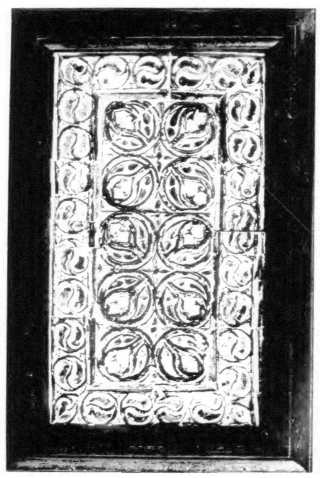

LUSTRED TILES

(Osma Collection)

POTTERY

jarrón. Fulfilling these conditions at all speed, he mounted the precious vessel on an ass, and briskly strode away. When he had gone a little distance the villagers, missing their cherished vase, though unaware, of course, of its artistic worth, swarmed angrily about the purchaser, flourished their knives and sticks at him, and pelted him with stones. At this he called upon the mayor for protection ; the mayor provided him with two armed men for body-guard, and, thus defended, the indomitable dealer reached Madrid and sold his jar to government for fifteen hundred dollars. Its present value is estimated at not less than thirty thousand.[1]

One of the earliest and most interesting notices relating to the preparation of this lustred ware is contained in a description by one of the royal archers, named Henry Cock, of the progress, performed in 1585, of Philip the Second from the court of Spain to Zaragoza.[2] Cock wrote of Muel, in Aragon :—" Almost all the inhabitants of this village are potters, and all the earthenware sold at Zaragoza is made in the following manner. The vessels are first fashioned to the required

[1] J. R. Mélida, *Jarrones arábigos de loza vidriada* : published in the *Boletín de la Sociedad Española de Excursionistas.*
[2] *Relación del viaje hecho por Felipe II. en* 1585. Madrid, 1876.

shape from a certain substance extracted from the earth of this locality. They are next baked in a specially constructed oven, and when removed from this are varnished with white varnish and polished, after which they are washed with a mixture of twenty-five pounds of lead, three or four pounds of tin, and as many pounds of a certain sand which is found there. All these ingredients are mixed into a paste resembling ice, which is broken small, pounded like flour, and kept in powder. This powder is mixed with water, the dishes are passed through it, and after being rebaked they keep their lustre. Next, in order to gild the pottery, they take the strongest vinegar mixed with about two *reales* of powdered silver, vermilion, and red ochre, and a little wire. When all is thoroughly mixed they paint the patterns on the dishes with a feather, bake them again, and their gold colour is now quite permanent. I was told all this by the potters themselves."[1]

Another most interesting account of the manu-

[1] The village of Muel continued to be a centre of this craft. Townsend, who travelled in Spain in 1786 and 1787, wrote of it:—" There are many potters, who turn their own wheels, not by hand, but with their feet, by means of a larger wheel concentric with that on which they mould the clay, and nearly level with the floor."

LXII

176

HISPANO-MORESQUE LUSTRED WARE

(A.D. 1460-1480. Osuna Collection)

POTTERY

facture of lustred ware was discovered in manuscript by Riaño in the British Museum, and,
although it belongs to a later date (1785), is well
worth quoting fully. It consists of a report upon
the later gilded pottery of Manises, and was drawn
up by order of the Count of Floridablanca :—

"After the pottery is baked, it is varnished with
white and blue, the only colours used besides the
gold lustre; the vessels are again baked; if the
objects are to be painted with gold colour, this
can only be put on the white varnish, after they
have gone twice through the oven. The vessels
are then painted with the said gold colour and
are baked a third time, with only dry rosemary
for fuel.

"The white varnish used is composed of lead
and tin, which are melted together in an oven
made on purpose; after these materials are
sufficiently melted, they become like earth, and
when in this state the mixture is removed and
mixed with an equal quantity in weight of sand :
fine salt is added to it, it is boiled again, and when
cold, pounded into powder. The only sand which
can be used is from a cave at Benalguacil, three
leagues from Manises. In order that the varnish
should be fine, for every *arroba*, twenty-five pounds

of lead, six to twelve ounces of tin must be added, and half a bushel of finely-powdered salt : if a coarse kind is required, it is sufficient to add a very small quantity of tin, and three or four *cuartos* worth of salt, which in this case must be added when the ingredient is ready for varnishing the vessel.

" Five ingredients enter into the composition of the gold colour : copper, which is better the older it is ; silver, as old as possible ; sulphur ; red ochre ; and strong vinegar, which are mixed in the following proportions : of copper three ounces, of red ochre twelve ounces, of silver one *peseta* (about a shilling), sulphur three ounces, vinegar a quart ; three pounds (of twelve ounces) of the earth or scoriæ, which is left after this pottery is painted with the gold colour, is added to the other ingredients.

" They are mixed in the following manner : a small portion of sulphur in powder is put into a casserole with two small bits of copper, between them a coin of one silver *peseta* ; the rest of the sulphur and copper is then added to it. When this casserole is ready, it is placed on the fire, and is made to boil until the sulphur is consumed, which is evident when no flame issues from it.

LXIII

HISPANO-MORESQUE LUSTRED WARE

(A.D. 1460–1480, Osma Collection)

POTTERY

The preparation is then taken from the fire, and when cold is pounded very fine; the red ochre and scoriæ are then added to it; it is mixed up by hand and again pounded into powder. The preparation is placed in a basin and mixed with enough water to make a sufficient paste to stick on the sides of the basin; the mixture is then rubbed on the vessel with a stick; it is therefore indispensable that the water should be added very gradually until the mixture is in the proper state.

"The basin ready prepared must be placed in an oven for six hours. At Manises it is customary to do so when the vessels of common pottery are baked; after this the mixture is scratched off the sides of the basin with some iron instrument; it is then removed from there and broken up into small pieces, which are pounded fine in a hand-mortar with the quantity of vinegar already mentioned, and after having been well ground and pounded together for two hours the mixture is ready for decorating. It is well to observe that the quantity of varnish and gold-coloured mixture which is required for every object can only be ascertained by practice."

Nevertheless, the gilded ware of the kingdom of Valencia had by this time deteriorated very greatly. Formerly, from as far back as the reign of Jayme the Conqueror, the other towns or villages of this region which produced the lustred and non-lustred pottery were Játiva, Paterna, Quarte, Vilallonga, Alaqua, Carcer, and Moncada. Early in the fourteenth century fourteen potteries were working in the town of Biar, and twenty-three at Traiguera. Manises, however, maintained the lead for many years. The notices of Eximenes and other writers concerning the pottery of this town have been already quoted. The same ware is mentioned in the sixteenth and seventeenth centuries by Diago (1613), Francisco Jávier Borrell, Beuter, and Martin de Viciana. Marineus Siculus, the chronicler of Ferdinand and Isabella, adds that similar or identical pottery ("*desta misma arte*") was made in Murcia, whose manufacture of it had been praised in earlier times by Ibn-Said. Toledo also manufactured gilded ware with blue or bistre colouring. García Llansó says that in the sixteenth century this capital produced plates which contain the arms of Spain in the centre, the rest of the plate being completely covered with minute geometrical or floral ornamentation.

It is certain that during the fourteenth and

LXIV

HISPANO-MORESQUE LUSTRED WARE

(*A.D.* 1460-1480. *Osma Collection*)

POTTERY

fifteenth centuries large quantities of lustred pottery were produced in many parts of Andalusia, Castile, Aragon, and Valencia. The oldest and most valuable specimens of this pottery are those which have the palest and most purely golden lustre, combined with blue or bluish decoration in the form of animals, coats of arms, or foliage. The lustred ware of Manises began to deteriorate about the time of the expulsion of the Moriscos, when the leaves and fronds of a clean gold tone upon a lightish ground are replaced by commoner and coarser patterns, and the gold itself by the coppery lustre which is still employed.

After the seventeenth century the further decline of this once famous industry may be traced from the accounts of travellers. Towards the middle of this century Bowles wrote that "two leagues from the capital (Valencia) is a fair-looking town of only four streets, whose occupants are nearly all potters. They make a *copper-coloured* ware of great beauty, *used for common purposes and for decorating the houses of the working-people of the province.* They make this ware of an argillaceous earth resembling in its colour and composition that portion of the soil of Valencia which produces native mercury. . . . The objects they fashion of this earth possess a glitter and are very inexpensive, since I purchased half a dozen plates for a *real*. Nevertheless, *this is not the ware which has the highest reputation in the kingdom of Valencia.* The factory which the Count of Aranda has established at Alcora is not surpassed in Europe, and is ahead of many in fineness of substance, hardness of the varnish, and elegance of form. It would be perfect of its kind if the varnish did not crack and peel off so easily."

According to Laborde, early in the nineteenth century Manises contained two potteries "of considerable extent, which employ seventy workmen. The people occupied in these possess the art of producing a gold *bronze* colour which they carefully keep a secret, never communicating it to any person." Elsewhere in the same book Laborde is more explicit. "Manises is a village situated a league and a quarter north of Valencia. It is seen on the left coming from New Castile. It is noted for its manufactories of earthen ware, which employ thirty kilns, and occupy a great part of the inhabitants. The women are employed in forming the designs and applying the colours. There are two large manufactories of a superior kind, the earthen ware of which is tolerably fine, of a beauti-

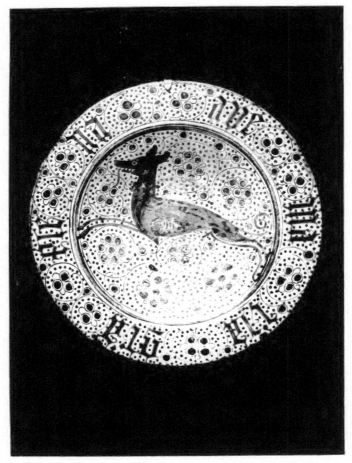

LXV

182

HISPANO-MORESQUE LUSTRED WARE

(Late 15th Century. Osma Collection)

ful white, and a moderate price. They also make here vases worked with a great degree of delicacy.

"The society of these workmen possess the secret of the composition of a colour which in the fire takes the tint and brightness of a beautiful gilt *bronze*. It has been unsuccessfully attempted to be imitated; the heads of the society compose the colour themselves, and distribute it to the masters who take care of it; it is a liquid of the colour of Spanish tobacco, but a little deeper."

The quantity of Hispano-Moresque lustred pottery preserved in the public and private collections of various countries is far from small, although to classify it according to the place and date of its production is nearly always a matter of extreme difficulty.

Among the earliest specimens are the vase of the Alhambra, those which are now in the museums of Palermo and Madrid, that which belonged to Fortuny, and the plaque which once was also his, and now forms part of the Osma collection. Lustred Spanish tiles are scarce. A few exist at Seville[1] and Granada, chiefly in altar-

[1] No direct proof has been found that lustred ware was ever made at Seville; but a document copied by Gestoso, and which I have already mentioned (p. 152), records that the famous *ollero*

fronts, along the archivolts of doorways, or, with heraldic motives, on the inner walls of houses of the aristocracy. Invariably, says Gestoso, such tiles are coloured with combinations of white, blue, and gold, since in the lustre process other colours—black, or green, or deepish yellow— proved unsatisfactory. Other lustred tiles of exquisite beauty are owned by Señor Osma, (Plate lxi.), and seem to have even gained in brilliance by the centuries that have passed over them. Riaño gives a list of the specimens of this pottery which are at South Kensington, consisting of bowls, vases, and plates. One of the vases is particularly beautiful. It dates from the fifteenth century, and is described by Fortnum as having "a spherical body on a trumpet-shaped base, with a neck of elongated funnel form, flanked by two large wing-shaped handles perforated with circular holes. The surface, except the mouldings, is entirely covered with a diaper-pattern of ivy or briony leaves, tendrils, and small flowers in brownish lustre and blue on the white ground."

Through the courtesy of Señor Osma I am

of the time of Ferdinand and Isabella, named Fernan Martinez Guijarro, reserved a department ("*tiendas del dorado*") of his premises for making or for storing lustred pottery.

LXVI

124   HISPANO-MORESQUE LUSTRED WARE

(Late 15th Century. Osma Collection)

POTTERY

able to give illustrations of a few of the finest specimens of lustred ware in his magnificent collection (Plates lxii.–lxvi.). The three small vessels facing pages 176, 178, and 180 are of Valencian workmanship, and date, according to their owner, from between 1460 and 1480. The two plates are also Valencian. The one with a bull in the centre dates from between 1480 and 1500; and that which has a greyhound from slightly earlier—say 1470 to 1490.

POTTERY OF SEVILLE, PUENTE DEL ARZOBISPO, TALAVERA DE LA REINA, TOLEDO, AND BARCE- LONA; POROUS WARE; PORCELAIN OF ALCORA AND THE ROYAL FACTORY OF THE BUEN RETIRO.

We have seen that Seville was an early and important centre of the potter's craft in Spain. Her potteries were celebrated even with the Romans, and probably have at no moment been inactive. Fifty, established in the suburb of Triana, were mentioned in the sixteenth century by Pedro de Medina, and documents which tell of many more have recently been discovered by Gestoso. The excellence of the Seville tiles has been described in a preceding section of this chapter. Their production still continues upon a large scale ; and the ware of the Cartuja factory, which reached the zenith of its fame towards the end of the eighteenth century, is considered by Jacquemart and other authorities to rival with the Italian wares of Savona.

Pottery made in other parts of the Peninsula —particularly that of Talavera de la Reina—is known to have been imitated by the Seville potters with embarrassing perfection. In the case of the so-called "loza de Puente del Arzobispo," it is the Seville ware itself which seems to have been imitated. Puente del Arzobispo is a small village near Toledo. Mendez wrote of it in the seventeenth century :—" Fine pottery is manufactured in about eight kilns, which produce more than 40,000 ducats yearly." " In 1755," says Riaño, " thirteen pottery kilns existed at this place ; they still worked in 1791, but their productions were very inferior in artistic merit."

Not many years ago the name of Puente del Arzobispo was connected by Baron Davillier with certain polychrome non-lustred plates and other vessels which are greatly esteemed for their rarity, and of which a few specimens exist in the South Kensington and other museums, as well as in one

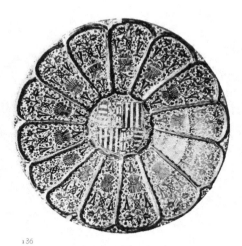

LXVII

136

HISPANO-MORESQUE LUSTRED WARE

POTTERY

or two private collections, such as that of Señor Osma.

Gestoso says that the usual diameter of these plates is either twenty-three centimetres or forty-two centimetres. "Their decoration, betraying at a glance the Saracenic influence, consists of leaves and flowers, together with animals of a more or less fantastic character : lions, rabbits, and birds. In other specimens the centre is occupied by a heart, fleurs-de-lis, or other fancy devices, or yet, in some few cases, with the head of a man or woman. These central designs are surrounded with leaves and flowers. The draughts-manship upon these plates is of the rudest, and the process of their colouring was as follows. The figures were drawn upon the unfired surface in manganese ink mixed with a greasy substance ; and after this the aqueous enamel or glaze was allowed to drop from a hogshair brush into the spaces which the black had outlined."

This will be recognized as the *cuerda seca* process, so extensively employed in making Seville tiles. Nevertheless, judging by certain marks upon this pottery, Baron Davillier declared it to proceed from Puente del Arzobispo. The marks in question consist in one or two examples of what appears to be the letters A.P. or P.A.[1] Davillier, however, affirmed that he had seen a plate fully inscribed as follows :—

The existence of this plate is now discredited ; at least, no trace of it can be discovered at this day.

[1] These, says Señor Osmo, are doubtful in every case, and are only found on plates which bear the figure of a lion. Two plates

in this gentleman's possession are thus marked , and

another

POTTERY

Upon the other hand, Gestoso points to various objects manufactured by the *cuerda seca* method, and which undoubtedly proceed from Seville. Among them are three shields, one of which, containing the arms of Ferdinand and Isabella, is of exceptional interest, for it is accompanied by an inscribed slab, evidently coeval with the shield itself, recording it to have been made in the year 1503, and by Jerónimo Suarez. This shield and slab were removed from a courtyard of the old Alhóndiga to Seville Museum, where they now remain. Of the two other shields, one belongs to Señor Osma, and the second, which is still at Seville, adorns the tomb of Don León Enriquez in the church of Santa Paula; and since it is un-questionable that all these *cuerda seca* shields, as well as quantities of *cuerda seca* tiles, were made at Seville, Gestoso prudently suggests that we should designate as "*cuerda seca* ware" that pottery which has hitherto passed as specially belonging to Puente del Arzobispo. In fact, towards the end of the fifteenth century this pottery is found extending northward from Seville to Toledo, and Señor Osma assures me that Toledo specimens are of a somewhat later manufacture than those which were produced at Seville. One of the rarest and most interesting *cuerda seca* plates in this gentleman's collection is reproduced herewith (lxviii.). No other plate of similar pattern is known to exist. Its date may be placed between 1480 and 1495, and it gives a curious illustration of the masculine headdress and headwear in the reign of Ferdinand and Isabella.

The pottery of Talavera de la Reina was at one time much esteemed. The earliest mention of it, says Riaño, occurs in 1560, in a manuscript history of this town, while another notice, dated 1576, says that here was produced "fine white glazed earthenware and other pottery, which supplied the country, part of Portugal, and India." More explicit are the observations of Father Alonso de Ajofrín, who wrote, in 1651, a history of Talavera. He says that "her pottery is as good as that of Pisa, while quantities of *azulejos* are made here to adorn the front of altars, churches, gardens, alcoves, saloons, and bowers, and large and small specimens of every kind. Two hundred workmen work at eight separate kilns. Four other kilns produce the commoner kinds of ware. Red porous clay vessels and drinking-cups are baked in two other kilns in a thousand shapes to imitate birds and other

DISH

Christo Islam now lustred ware in the Cuerda seca style.
A.D. 14—? 15?.   (Osma Collection)

creatures; also *brinquiños* for the use of ladies, so deliciously flavoured that after drinking the water they contained, they eat the cup in which it was brought them."

The following most interesting notice relating to this town is also quoted by Riaño: "The earthenware pottery made here has reached a great perfection; it is formed of white and red clay. Vases, cups, *bucaros* and *brinquiños* are made of different kinds, dishes and table centres, and imitations of snails, owls, dogs, and every kind of fruits, olives, and almonds. These objects are painted with great perfection, and the imitations of porcelain brought from the Portuguese Indies are most excellent. Everyone is surprised that in so small a town such excellent things should be made. The varnish used for the white pottery is made with tin and sand, and is now found to be more acceptable than coloured earthenware; so much so, that persons of importance who pass by this town, although they have in their houses dinner-services of silver, buy earthenware made at Talavera, on account of its excellence. The sand which was used to make the white varnish was brought from Hita, and is now found at Mejorada, near

Talavera.   This sand is as fine and soft as silk.

" The red pottery made at Talavera is much to be commended, for besides the great variety of objects, and the different medals which they place upon them, they have invented some small *brinquiños* of so small and delicate a kind, that the ladies wear them.   Rosaries are also made of the same material.   A certain scent is added in the manufacture of this pottery which excites the appetite and taste of the women, who eat the pottery so frequently that it gives great trouble to their confessors to check this custom."

This porous pottery for keeping water cool had been imported from America, and was chiefly made in Andalusia, Portugal, and Extremadura. It is still produced at Andujar and elsewhere. Nearly all travellers in Spain describe it, and insist upon the curious circumstance that it was eaten by the Spanish women.   " I have mentioned elsewhere," wrote Countess d'Aulnoy, "the longing many women feel to chew this clay, which often obstructs their bodies internally.   Their stomachs swell, and grow as hard as stone, while their skin turns yellow as a quince.   I also felt a curiosity to taste this ware, that is so highly yet

AN *ALFARERÍA* OR POTTER'S YARD

(Granada)

so undeservedly esteemed ; but I would devour a grindstone rather than put it in my mouth again. Nevertheless, if one wants to be agreeable to the Spanish ladies, one has to present them with some *bucaros*, which they themselves call *barros*, and which, as many deem, possess such numerous and admirable qualities, since they claim for the clay that it cures sickness, and that a drinking vessel made of it betrays the presence of a poison. I possess one which spoils the taste of wine, but greatly improves water. This liquid seems to boil and tremble when it is thrown into the cup in question ; but after a little while the vessel empties—so porous is the clay of which it is composed—and then it has a fragrant odour."

Similar accounts are given by travellers of a later time. " I wish, " wrote Swinburne, " I could contrive a method of carrying you some of the fine earthen jars, called *buxaros*, which are made in Andalusia. They are remarkably convenient for water-drinkers, as they are light, smooth, and handy ; being not more than half-baked, they are very porous, and the outside is kept moist by the water's filtering through ; though placed in the sun, the water in the pots remains as cold as ice. The most disagreeable circumstance attending them is, that they emit a smell of earth refreshed by a sudden shower after a long drought."[1]

Laborde, who wrote a few years later, seems to have copied some of his information from Bowles. "The Murcians," he said, "use in their houses little jars called *Bucaros*, the same as those which in some parts of Andalusia are called Alcarrazas.[2] They have handles open at the top, are smaller at the bottom than above, and bulge in the middle; they are slight, porous, smooth, and half-baked; they are made of a peculiar kind of clay. When water is put into them, they emit a smell like that sent up by the earth after a shower of rain in summer. The water makes its way very slowly through the pores, and keeps them constantly moist on the outside; they are used to cool water for drinking. The windows and balconies of all

---

[1] *Travels through Spain*; p. 305. Swinburne could have been no lover of nature to speak in such terms of the smell of earth.

[2] One of the prettiest of the popular Spanish *coplas* has the *alcarraza* for its theme;—

> "Alcarraza de tu casa
> chiquilla, quisiera ser,
> para besarte los labios
> cuando fueras á beber."

"Dearest, I would be the *alcarraza* in your house; so should I kiss your lips each time you drank from me."

194

POTTERY

the houses have large iron rings, with a flat surface, on which they are placed at night, and the water, oozing incessantly, becomes very cool.[1] In Andalusia some of these jars are white, and others red ; in Murcia they have only white ones. They appear to be in every respect of the same nature as the evaporating vases of Africa, Egypt, Syria, and India, of which so much has been said by travellers, and on which the learned have made so many dissertations."

The same vessels are noticed by Ford in his description of a Spanish *posada*. "Near the staircase downstairs, and always in a visible place, is a gibbous jar, *tinaja*, of the ancient classical amphora shape, filled with fresh water ; and by it is a tin or copper utensil to take water out with, and often a row of small pipkins, made of a red porous clay,[2] which are kept ready filled with water, on, or rather in, a shelf fixed to the wall,

[1] Laborde's translator adds : "These jars are very common in Jamaica ; they are of different sizes, from a pint to three pints. A number of them are ranged at night in the balconies, to furnish a supply of cool water. Coolers of a similar kind have been lately introduced in England."

[2] "Those of the finest quality," adds Ford, "are called *Bucaros* ; the best come from South America —the form is more elegant, the clay finer, and often sweet-scented ; many women have a trick of biting, even eating bits of them."

and called *la tallada, el taller.* These pots, *alcarrazas,* from the constant evaporation, keep the water extremely cool. They are of various shapes, many, especially in Valencia and Andalusia, being of the unchanged identical form of those similar clay drinking-vessels discovered at Pompeii. They are the precise *trulla.* Martial speaks both of the colour and the material of those made at Saguntum, where they still are prepared in great quantities; they are not unlike the *ckool'lehs* of Egypt, which are made of the same material and for the same purposes, and represent the ancient Canobic στατικα. They are seldom destined to be placed on the table; their bottoms being pointed and conical, they could not stand upright. This singular form was given to the *vasa futilia,* or cups used at the sacrifices of Vesta, which would have been defiled had they touched the ground. As soon, therefore, as they are drunk off, they are refilled and replaced in their holes on the shelf, as is done with decanters in our butlers' pantries."[1]

I am only aware of one author who derides the statement that this porous clay was eaten by the Spanish women. According to Bowles, who cer-

[1] *Handbook*; Vol. I., p. 26.

POTTERY

tainly describes and comments on it with intelligence and scholarship, the neighbourhood of Andujar contains "large quantities of the white argil of which are made the jars or *alcarrazas* which serve in many parts of Spain for cooling water in the summer-time. In other parts of Andalusia is found a red variety of this clay, employed in making the vessels known as *búcaros*, which serve to freshen the water as well as for drinking it out of—a thing the Spanish ladies love greatly. Both the white *alcarrazas* and the *búcaros* as red as the blood of a bull are thin, porous, smooth, and half-baked. When filled with water they emit a pleasant smell like that of dry earth rained upon in summer, and as the water filters through the outer surface, remain continually damp." The same writer adds that at that time (1752) the *búcaros* proceeding from the Indies were of finer workmanship, and had a more agreeable smell than those of Spanish manufacture. "In the Encyclopædia," he continues, "and in the Dictionary of Natural History, we read that Spanish ladies are for ever chewing *búcaro*, and that the hardest penance their confessors can inflict upon them is to deprive them for a single day of this enjoyment." Bowles, however, quotes these observations in a scornful tone, and deprecates the habit of " believing writers who without inquiring into things, concoct and publish novels to divert the populace and rid them of their money."

Turning our attention once again to the finer kinds of Talavera ware, Gestoso adduces proofs that this as well as Chinese porcelain was faultlessly and freely imitated in the potteries of Seville. Here, therefore, is a source of fresh confusion ; and probably a great proportion of the polychrome ware which goes by the name of Talaveran is really of Sevillian origin. It is further known that at one period, which seems to begin with the second half of the sixteenth century, potters who were natives of Talavera were hired to work in Seville.

It has not been ascertained when Talavera herself grew celebrated for this industry. García Llansó supposes that at first, before it felt the influence of Italy and France, her pottery was partly Mudejar, and vestiges of oriental art survive in fairly late examples. The characteristic colour-scheme was either blue on white, or else the decoration is more variegated. Riaño says :— " Although we find by the remarks we have quoted from contemporary authors that earthenware of

every description was made at Talavera, the
specimens which are more generally met with may
be divided into two groups, which are painted on
a white ground, either in blue, or in colours, in the
manner of Italian maiolica. The most important
examples which have reached us consist of bowls
of different sizes, dishes, vases (Plate lxx.), *tinajas,*
holy-water vessels, medicine jars, and wall decoration. Blue oriental china was imitated to a vast
extent : the colouring was successful, but the design
was an imitation of the baroque school of the time,
and the figures, landscapes, and decoration follow
the bad taste so general in Spain in the eighteenth
century. The imitations of Italian maiolica are
effective. The colours most commonly used are
manganese, orange, blue, and green."

Talavera maintained her reputation for pottery
till nearly the middle of the eighteenth century,
supporting more than six hundred workmen
employed in eight large potteries.[1] From then

---

[1] "On y fait," wrote Alvarez de Colmenar, "des ouvrages
vernissés d'une façon ingénieuse, avec des peintures variées de bon
gôut ; on estime ces ouvrages autant que ceux de Pise et des Indes
Orientales, et on en fournit plusieurs provinces. Ce négoce rend
plus de cinquante mille ducats par an."—*Annales d'Espagne et de
Portugal* ; Vol. II., p. 187. This work is dated 1740, but my copy is
reprinted from another edition published earlier in the century.

onwards the trade declined, and by the close of the same century was practically dead, owing, Larruga tells us, to the constantly increasing cost of prime materials. Nevertheless, the Crown made efforts to revive the craft, and met with some success till 1777, in which year four establishments (locally known as *barrerías*) for making common pottery were opened in the same town, and speedily crushed their rivals. "The potteries of Talavera," wrote Laborde soon after this, "were greatly celebrated for many years, and supplied a lucrative and important branch of commerce. They are evidently on the decline. The manufactories are reduced to seven or eight. These productions no longer exhibit the same delicacy of execution. Their designs are also lamentably defective. The material employed in them is a certain earth which is found near Calera, three leagues from Talavera."

The older Talavera ware, decorated, as a rule, with horses, birds, hunting-scenes, or coats of arms, is seldom met with nowadays. Although it is not particularly choice, the drawing is firm, and the colouring vigorous and agreeable.

I have said that pottery continued to be made in Aragon, at Muel, Villafeliche, and other places.

POTTERY

In course of time these local industries were also suffered to decay. Laborde says that early in the nineteenth century the Villafeliche factory employed thirty-eight workmen. "The ware is of a very inferior sort. This article might be carried to a greater extent. In several parts of the province, earth is found of an excellent quality for earthenware, particularly in Zaragoza and in Tauste ; the latter affords the best, which is very fine, and of three colours, and would answer for the making of porcelain."

In the eighteenth century Toledo, upon the initiative of Don Ignacio Velasco, produced good imitations of Genoese ware, while other kinds of pottery were made at Teruel, Valladolid, Jaen, Zamora, Segovia, Puente del Arzobispo, and in the Balearic Islands. Another region which continued to be a most important centre of the potter's craft was Cataluña, where it had always been encouraged by this thrifty and art-loving people. As early as the year 1257 two potters occupied a place upon the municipal council of Barcelona, while the potters' guild was strictly regulated from the beginning of the fourteenth century.[1] At the

[1] For a sketch of the origin and growth of the Spanish trade guilds, see Appendix H.

same time two whole streets in the centre of the town, as well as others in the suburbs, were occupied by potters. The ancient names of these streets are yet retained in the Calles Escudillers, Escudillers Blancs (white varnished pottery), Obradors (where many of the potteries were situated), and Tallers (*i.e.* the potteries for producing common ware).

The pottery of Cataluña generally was largely exported to Sicily, Alexandria, and other parts. Among the places in this region which produced it were Tarragona, Tortosa, and Villafranca. In 1528 the municipal council of the capital herself forbade, as a protective measure, the introduction into Barcelona of local pottery made at Malgrat, La Selva, and other towns and villages of this neighbourhood. In 1546 the Portuguese Barreyros declared in his work *Chorografía de algunos lugares* that the Barcelona ware surpassed all other classes made in Spain, including the Valencian. She continued to produce good pottery all through the sixteenth century, and excellent common ware until considerably later.[1]

About the beginning of the eighteenth century

[1] *Historia General del Arte.*—Vol. II.: *Cerámica*, by García Llansó.

POTTERY

Laborde mentioned as working centres of this craft "manufactories of delf-ware at Avilés, Gijón, Oviedo, Nava, and Cangas de Onis, in the Asturias; at Segovia in Old Castile ; at Puente del Arzobispo and Talavera de la Reina in New Castile ; at Seville in the kingdom of that name ; at Villafeliche in Aragon ; at Onda, Alcora, and Manises, in the kingdom of Valencia ; at San Andero in Biscay ; and at Tortosa in Cataluña. . . . . The most important of these potteries is the one at Alcora, the delf of which is tolerably fine, though not of the first quality. No china is made, except at Alcora and Madrid : that of the former place is very common, and inconsiderable as to quantity. The china manufactured at Madrid is beautiful, and without exaggeration may be considered as equalling that of Sèvres. It is a royal pottery ; but it is impossible to give any description of its state, because admission to the interior of the manufactory is strictly prohibited."

Ricord states in his pamphlet relative to Valencian industries that in 1791 factories of high-class pottery were working in the kingdom of Valencia, at Onda, Alcora, Ribesalves, Manises, Eslida, and Bechí ; and of common ware at San Felipe, Morella, Manises, Murviedro, Alicante,

Moncada, Orihuela, Segorbe, and other towns and villages of this locality. In all, there were throughout the province eighty-seven of these latter potteries, besides two hundred and twenty tileries, and four factories of artistic tiles or *azulejos* established at Valencia. The yearly output of these *azulejerias* was 150,000 tiles, 20,000 of which were exported to Andalusia and Castile.

Although the pottery of Alcora only achieved distinction at a later age, this craft had long been practised in the neighbourhood. This circumstance induced the Count of Aranda to found here, in 1726, a large factory for producing costly and artistic ware. Riaño obtained permission to examine the archives of the family of Aranda, with their mass of documents relating to this enterprise. His notice of Alcora ware is therefore most complete and valuable, and has been copied, frequently without acknowledgment, by almost every writer on the subject.

It appears from these archives that the cost of building and opening the factory of Alcora amounted to about £10,000. The works were placed beneath the supervision of Don Joaquín Joseph de Sayas, at the same time that a French-

man named Ollery was engaged at a good salary
and brought from Moustiers to act as principal
draughtsman. A couple of years later Count
Aranda paid Ollery the high compliment of saying
that "the fine and numerous models which he
has designed, have contributed to make my manufacture the first in Spain." He seems to have
retired in 1737, when the Count rewarded him
with a yearly pension of five hundred francs
besides the amount of his salary, "for his especial
zeal in the improvement of the manufactory, and
his great skill in directing the construction of every
kind of work." Riaño adds that from this date
until the manufacture of porcelain in 1764, only
Spanish artists worked at Alcora.

The products of this factory continued to
improve, and reached, in course of time, a yearly
total of about three hundred thousand objects.
The ordinances, which are dated between 1732
and 1733, tell us that "in these works of ours no
pottery should be made except the very finest,
similar to the Chinese, and of as fine an earth.
The models and wheels should be perfect, the
drawing first-rate, the varnish and colours excellent, and the pottery light and of the highest
quality, for it is our express wish that the best

pottery should only be distinguished from that of an inferior kind by the greater or less amount of painting which covers it."

Not less interesting are certain communications, copied by Riaño, which passed in 1746 between the Spanish Tribunal of Commerce and the Count of Aranda, in which it is stated that "the perfection of the earthenware of Alcora consists in the excellent models which have been made by competent foreign artists, as well as in the quality of the earth and the recipes brought at great cost from abroad." We learn from the same document that "from the earliest period of the manufacture, pyramids with figures of children, holding garlands of flowers and baskets of fruits on their heads, were made with great perfection ; also brackets, centre and three-cornered tables, large objects, some as large as five feet high, to be placed upon them, chandeliers, cornucopias, statues of different kinds, and animals of different sorts and sizes. The entire ornamentation of a room has also been made here ; the work is so perfect that nothing in Spain, France, Italy, or Holland could equal it in merit."

It is not necessary to follow in close detail all the modifications and vicissitudes (extending

over quite a hundred years) which affected the
Alcora factory. I therefore only take some
general notices from Riaño. In 1750 Count
Aranda transferred the works to a private company, which remained in possession of them until
1766. In 1741 a Frenchman named François
Haly was engaged for ten years, and with a
yearly salary of rather more than a thousand
francs, under the following conditions :—

"That the travelling expenses of his wife and
children should be given him, and that his salary
should be paid as soon as he made before the
Director and two competent judges the different
kinds of porcelain which he had undertaken to
make." Haly agreed to surrender his recipes,
and it was promised him that he should have two
modellers and one painter working by his side,
and that if in one year his porcelain were satisfactory, the Count would make him a present of a
thousand *tornoises*.[1]

Porcelain was first produced at Alcora towards
the middle of the eighteenth century. A contract was drawn up on March 24th, 1764, with
a German called John Christian Knipfer, who
had already worked there in the pottery section.

[1] Riaño; *Handbook*; pp. 182, 183.

By the original agreement, which exists in the archives, we find he was to prepare works of " porcelain and painting similar to those made at Dresden, during a period of six years, under the following conditions :—

" That the said Knipfer obliges himself to make and teach the apprentices the composition and perfection of porcelain paste, its varnishes, and colours, and whatever he may know at the present time, or discover during this period of six years ; he is not to prevent the Director of the Works from being present at all the essays made.

" The said Knipfer offers to make and varnish porcelain, and to employ gold and silver in its decoration, and in that of the ordinary wares ; likewise the colours of crimson, purple, violet, blues of different shades, yellow, greens, browns, reds, and black.

" That Knipfer will give up an account of his secrets, and the management and manner of using them, in order that in all times the truth of what he has asserted may be verified."

In 1774 a Frenchman named François Martin was engaged to make " hard paste porcelain, Japanese faïence, English paste (pipeclay), and likewise to mould and bake it : the necessary materials

LXXI

ORNAMENT IN PORCELAIN OF THE
BUEN RETIRO

to be provided by the Count of Aranda." Riaño
says that the combined assistance of Knipfer and
Martin went far to better the products of the factory.

Martin died in 1786, and Knipfer left soon afterwards. A Frenchman was now engaged, whose
services proved also beneficial to the works.
This was Pierre Cloostermans, "a skilful man,
well versed in the manufacture of porcelain pastes,
as well as in painting and decorating them."
Cloostermans, however, was much molested by
the envy of the Spanish workmen at Alcora, as
well as by their typical intolerance in matters of
religion, although the Count, his master, behaved
towards him with the utmost kindness. Under
his supervision, the quality of Alcora ware was
notably improved. Figures and groups of many
kinds were attempted, and even Wedgwood jasper
ware was creditably imitated. In 1789, among
other pottery that was sent to Madrid were "two
hard paste porcelain cups, adorned with low relief
in the English style." The most important one
was moulded by Francisco Garcés, the garlands
and low reliefs by Joaquín Ferrer, sculptor, the
flowers on the covers by an apprentice, helped
by Cloostermans.

Dated in the same year (1789), Riaño quotes an

interesting letter from the Count of Aranda to Don Pedro Abadia, his steward. " I wish," he said, " to export the porcelain of my manufactory, but chiefly in common objects, such as cups of different kinds, tea and coffee services, etc. These may be varied in form and colour, the principal point being that the paste should bear hot liquids, for we Spaniards above everything wish that nothing we buy should ever break. By no means let time be wasted in making anything that requires much loss of time. The chief object is that the pastes should be of first-rate excellence and durability."

In 1793 Cloostermans was driven from the country by political disturbances; but he was allowed to return in 1795, and resumed his duties at the factory. All through these years Alcora continued to make most excellent pottery. Essays were made with foreign earths, as well as with the best that could be found in Spain. About this time kaolin was discovered in Cataluña, and the Count was particularly anxious that this native product should be utilised at Alcora. "The kaolin of Cataluña," he wrote in 1790, "may be good or bad, but it is acknowledged to be kaolin, and if we do not employ it I must close my works."

The Count of Aranda and Pierre Cloostermans

POTTERY

both died in 1798, and in 1800 the Duke of Hijar became the manager and proprietor of the potteries. " Two hundred workmen were employed, and pottery of every description was made, common earthenware, pipeclays in imitation of the English ones, and porcelain in small quantities; common wares were made in large quantities; the pipe-clays were pronounced superior to the English in brilliancy, but were so porous that they were easily stained. A large number of snuff-boxes and other small objects belong to this period."—(Riaño.)

In the early years of the nineteenth century Alcora ware deteriorated not a little. This decline was further aggravated by the French invasion ; and although an attempt was subsequently made to revive the industry by bringing craftsmen from the porcelain factory of Madrid, it suffered fresh relapses and produced henceforward little but the commonest kinds of ware. " This system," says Riaño, "continued until 1858, when the Duke of Hijar sold the manufactory to Don Ramón Girona, who brought over English workmen from Staffordshire in order to improve the wares. Many imitations of the older styles have also been made at Alcora of late years."

Riaño appends instructive tables, which I copy

in Appendix 1, of every kind of pottery manufactured at Alcora. He also believes that a great
deal of pottery which was formerly thought to
proceed from French or English factories is really
of Alcora make, including "a great quantity of
objects of white pipeclay porcelain which have
been found of late years in Spain. They have
hitherto been classified by amateurs as Leeds
pottery. We find, in papers relating to Alcora,
that a decided distinction is made between white
and straw-coloured pottery. This indication may
be sufficient to distinguish it from English wares."

The celebrated Royal Porcelain Factory of the
Buen Retiro at Madrid, formerly situated in the
public gardens of that name and popularly known
as the "Fabrica de la China," was founded in
1759 by Charles the Third, who erected a vast
edifice for this purpose, and filled it with a multi-
tude of workmen and their families, including two
hundred and twenty-five persons whom he brought
over from his other factory of Capo-di-Monte in
Italy. He also transferred a great part of the
material.[1] The cost of the new works amounted
to eleven and a half millions of *reales*, and they

[1] On September 11th, 1759, the king wrote to his Secretary of
State, Richard Wall :—"The workmen and utensils of the Royal

were terminated in 1764. The cost of keeping up the factory is stated by Larruga to have amounted to three millions of *reales* yearly. The first directors were Juan Tomás Bonicelli and Domingo Bonicelli, and the first modellers-in-chief and superintendents, possessing the secrets of the fabrication (*secretistas*), were Cayetano Schepers and Carlos Gricci.

Riaño says that every kind of porcelain was made at the Buen Retiro, "hard and soft paste, white china, glazed or unglazed, or painted and modelled in the style of Capo-di-Monte. A great many objects existed imitating the blue jasper ware of Wedgwood, and they also made flowers, coloured and biscuit, groups (Pl. lxxi.), and single figures, and painted porcelain of different kinds. Great quantities of tiles for pavements were also made there, which may still be seen at the Casa del Labrador at Aranjuez : they are mentioned in the accounts which exist at the Ministry of Finance for 1807 and 1808. We find in these same accounts interesting details of the objects made monthly.

Porcelain Manufactory of Capo-di-Monte must also be sent from Naples to Alicante, in the vessels prepared for this purpose, in order to proceed from Alicante to Madrid. The necessary conveyances are to be provided, and the expenses to be charged to his Majesty's account."

ARTS AND CRAFTS OF OLDER SPAIN

In January, 1808, a large number of figures were made, including 151 heads for the table centre which was made for the king, 306 objects ornamented with paintings, 2506 tiles, 577 objects of less artistic importance, such as dishes, plates, etc. The finest specimens which exist are in the Neapolitan style, and are two rooms at the palaces of Madrid and Aranjuez, of which the walls are completely covered with China plaques and looking-glasses, modelled in the most admirable manner with figures, fruits, and flowers. The room at Aranjuez is covered with a bold ornamentation of figures in the Japanese style, in high relief, painted with colours and gold with the most exquisite details. The figures unite the fine Italian modelling with the Japanese decoration. The chandelier is in the same style (Plate lxxii.). Upon a vase on the wainscot to the right of the entrance door is the following inscription :—

JOSEPH
GRICCI
DELINEAV^{it}
ET
SCUL.^{it}
1763.

LXXII

ROOM DECORATED WITH PORCELAIN OF THE BUEN RETIRO

(Royal Palace of Aranjuez)

POTTERY

This same date is repeated in the angles, and in some shields near the roof we find,

AÑO

1765;

probably the year the work was terminated."

The earliest mark upon the Buen Retiro porcelain was a blue fleur-de-lis, to which were subsequently added the letter M and a royal crown. Still later, in the reign of Charles the Fourth, the mark used was a fleur-de-lis with two crossed C's.

The object of the Buen Retiro Factory was almost wholly to supply the Crown with costly ware, and would-be visitors were jealously excluded. Townsend wrote in 1786: "I tried to obtain admission to the china manufacture, which is likewise administered on the king's account, but his Majesty's injunctions are so severe, that I could neither get introduced to see it, nor meet with anyone who had ever been able to procure that favour for himself. I was the less mortified upon this occasion, because from the specimens which I have seen, both in the palace at Madrid and in the provinces, it resembles the manufacture of Sèvres, which I had formerly visited in a tour through France."

Laborde also complained that the factory was " wholly inaccessible : all entrance to it is interdicted, and its existence is only ascertained by the exhibition which is made of its productions in the royal palace." The same writer refers to another class of work which was produced here, namely, stone mosaic. "The process by which stone is wrought into pictures is as delicate as it is curious : a selection is made from marble fragments of various shades and dimensions, which are found, by judicious assimilation, to produce no bad resemblance to painting." Jean François de Bourgoing, French Minister at Madrid, was lucky enough, in 1782, to penetrate into the factory and view the process. " Le Monarque actuel," he wrote, "a établi dans leur intérieur une fabrique de porcelaine, dont l'entrée est jusqu'à présent interdite à tout le monde. On veut sans doute que ses essais se perfectionnent dans le silence, avant de les exposer aux regards des curieux. Ses productions ne peuvent encore se voir que dans les Palais du Souverain, ou dans quelques Cours d'Italie, auxquelles il les envoie en présens. On travaille dans le même édifice à certains ouvrages de marqueterie, qui sont encore peu connus en Europe. J'y pénétrai

POTTERY

un jour, sous les auspices d'un étranger distingué en faveur duquel le Roi avoit levé la prohibition rigoureuse, qui en exclut tout le monde. Je suis témoin de la patience and de l'adresse avec lesquelles on taille and on rapproche divers petits morceaux de marbre coloré, pour en former des tableaux assez compliqués, qui en faisant à-peu-près le même effet que la peinture, ont sur elle l'avantage de braver par leur couleur immortelles les ravages du temps, qui n'épargnent pas les plus belles productions de cet art." [1]

This factory was not long-lived. Until 1803 it followed the styles of the older establishment at Capo-di-Monte, uniting neo-classic motives with the manner of Baroque. In that year it began to produce porcelain imitating that of Sèvres, and two Frenchmen, Vivien and Victor Perche, were brought from Paris to superintend this change. "Among the finest specimens of this period," says Riaño, "are a splendid clock and four vases, two mètres high, with porcelain flowers, which exist in one of the state rooms of the Palace of Madrid. The vases are placed in the four corners of the room. The clock is ornamented with large biscuit figures. A large number of

[1] *Nouveau Voyage en Espagne*; Vol. I., pp. 232, 233.

vases of Retiro china exist at the royal palaces of Madrid, Aranjuez, and the Escorial. They are often finely mounted in gilt bronze with muslin or porcelain flowers. The blue of the imitations of Wedgwood is not so pure, nor is the biscuit work so fine as the English. Gold is often added to these specimens."

Nevertheless, this manufacture was by now decadent. It had suffered severely from the death of Charles the Third, and upon the French invasion in 1808 was seized by the enemy and occupied by them for several months. During the reign of the "*intruso*," Joseph Buonaparte, porcelain was still produced to some extent; but by the time of the Peninsular campaign the works had practically ceased. "Near this quarter," wrote Ford, describing the Retiro gardens, towards the middle of last century, "was *La China*, or the royal porcelain manufactory, that was destroyed by the invaders, and made by them into a fortification, which surrendered, with two hundred cannon, August 14th, 1812, to the Duke. It was blown up October 30th, by Lord Hill, when the misconduct of Ballesteros compelled him to evacuate Madrid. Now *La China* is one of the standing Spanish and *afrancesado* calumnies against us, as

LXXIII

POTTERY

it is stated that we, the English, destroyed this manufactory from commercial jealousy, because it was a rival to our potteries. 'What can be done (as the Duke said) with such libels but despise them. There is no end of the calumnies against me and the army, and I should have no time to do anything else if I were to begin either to refute or even to notice them?' (Disp., Oct. 16, 1813.) These china potsherds and similar inventions of the enemy shivered against his iron power of conscious superiority.

"The real plain *truth* is this. The French broke the *ollas*, and converted this Sèvres of Madrid into a Bastile, which, and not the pipkins, was destroyed by the English, who now, so far from dreading any Spanish competition, have actually introduced their system of pottery; and accordingly very fair china is now made at Madrid and Seville, and by English workmen. At the latter place a convent, also converted by Soult into a citadel, is now made a hardware manufactory by our countryman, Mr Pickman. Ferdinand the Seventh, on his restoration, re-created *La China*, removing the workshops and warerooms to La Moncloa, once a villa of the Alva family on the Manzanares."

ARTS AND CRAFTS OF OLDER SPAIN

This factory of La Moncloa was founded in 1816, and it continued working until 1849. A specimen of the Moncloa ware is reproduced in Plate lxxiii.

Outside the royal palaces of Spain, the Buen Retiro porcelain is scarce. The choicest collections which are not the property of the Crown belong, or have belonged till recently, to the Marquis of Arcicollar, the Count of Valencia de Don Juan, and Don Francisco Laiglesia.

Glass

GLASS

SMALL vessels of uncoloured glass, belonging to the Celtic period, have been discovered in Galicia ; so that the origin of this industry in Spain is possibly pre-Roman. After the conquest glass was made here by the Romans,[1] who built their ovens with a celebrated argil (potter's earth) extracted from the neighbourhood of Valencia or Tortosa. The Roman glass was doubtless imitated by the native Spaniards : at least we know from observations by Saint Isidore that this substance was quite familiar to the Visigoths. " Olim fiebat et in Italia, et per Gallias, et Hispaniam arena alba mollissima pila mola qua terebatur." The same author speaks with admiration of coloured glass-work imitating precious stones. " Tingitur

[1] "Jam vero et per Gallias Hispaniasque simili modo harenæ temperantur."—Pliny, Bk. xxxvi ; Chap. 66.

The chief centres of glass-making were Tarragona, several towns of Betica (Andalusia), and the Balearic Islands.

etiam multis modis, ita ut hyacinthos, saphirosque et virides imitetur et oniches vel aliarum gemmarum colores"; and again; "Fingunt enim eas ex diverso genere nigro, candido, minioque colore. Nam pro lapide pretiosissimo smaragdo quidam vitrum arte inficiunt, et fallit oculos sub dolo quadam falsa irriditas quoadusque non est qui probet simulatum et arguat : sic et alia alio atque alio modo. Neque enim est sine fraude ulla vita mortalium." We gather from these statements that coloured glass in imitation of the genuine precious stone was freely manufactured by the Visigoths. Such imitations, justifying by their excellence Saint Isidore's assertion that "vera a falsis discernere magna difficultas est," may still be seen upon the crowns and other ornaments discovered at Guarrazar (see Vol. I., pp. 15–29), as well as upon triptyches and weapons. Indeed, a taste for imitation jewels forms an inherent trait of Spanish character, and is discoverable at all moments of the national history. Travellers have constantly observed it, and the remarks, already quoted, of Countess d'Aulnoy, are confirmed by other authors. "In the broken banks south of the river," wrote Swinburne of the Manzanares at Madrid, "are found large quantities of pebbles, called Diamonds

GLASS

of Saint Isidro. They cut them like precious stones, and ladies of the first fashion wear them in their hair as pins, or on their fingers as rings. They have little or no lustre, and a very dead glassy water. The value of the best rough stone does not exceed a few pence."

It is chiefly in the form of imitation gems that specimens of the earliest Spanish glass have been preserved until our time,[1] although the characteristic of old Roman glass which is known in Italian as the *lattocinio* or "milk-white" ornament, in the form of a thread or line carried all over the surface of a vessel, remains until this day a common feature of the glass of Spain, besides being found in Spanish-Moorish glass-work.

Rico y Sinobas says that the rules for cutting glass by means of a diamond or *naife* (as it was once called) are embodied in a treatise titled *El Lapidario*, originally written (perhaps in the fourth, fifth, or sixth century) in Hebrew, and

---

[1] The distinction which Riaño attempts to draw between glass and glass paste is unsatisfactory. He remarks, too, that the manufacture of glass *may* have existed in Spain at an earlier period than the last three centuries, but continues : "The earliest mention of glass-works in Spain will be found in Pliny, who, while explaining the proceedings which were employed in this industry, says that glass was made in a similar manner in France and Spain.

which was brought to Spain some two or three hundred years later. This treatise was translated into Arabic by one Abolais, who lived at some time previous to the thirteenth century, and subsequently (in the year 1248, and by command of Alfonso the Learned) into the Castilian language.

Mixed up with a great deal of fabulous and fantastic matter, this treatise contains instructive and interesting notices of the composition and the colouring of old glass, including that of Spain. One of such notices is the following. "Of the eleventh degree of the sign of Sagittarius is the glass stone, containing a substance which is a body in itself (sand), and another which is added to it (salt), and when they clean these substances and draw them from the fire, they make between the two a single body. The stone thus made (glass) has many colours. Sometimes it is white (and this is nobler and better than the others), or sometimes it is red, or green, or *xade* (a dark, burnt colour), or purple. It is a stone which readily melteth in the fire, but which, when drawn therefrom, turneth again to its former substance: and if it be drawn from the flame unseasonably, and without cooling it little by little, it snappeth asunder. And it receiveth readily whatever

GLASS

colour be placed upon it. And if an animal be hurt therewith, it openeth as keen a wound as though it were of iron."

The treatise also describes a stone called *ecce*, which was used in glassmaking, saying that it was found in Spain, "in a mountain, not of great height, which overlooks the town of Arraca, and is called Secludes. And the stone is of an intense black colour, spotted with yellow drops. It is shiny and porous, brittle, and of light weight . . . . and if it be ground up with honey, and the glass be smeared with it and submitted to the fire, it dyes the glass of a beautiful gold colour, and makes it stronger than it was before, so that it does not melt so readily, or snap asunder with such ease."

I have said that the power of a diamond to cut glass is referred to in the same work, which further tells us that this gem "breaketh all other kind of stones, boring holes in them or cutting them, and no other stone is able to bruise it; nay more, it powdereth all other stones if it be rubbed upon them . . . . and such as seek to cut or perforate those other stones take portions of a diamond, small and slender and sharp-pointed, and mount them on slips of silver or of copper, and with them make the holes or cuttings they require. Thus do they grave and carve intaglios."

All these branches of glassmaking were therefore practised by the Spaniards from an early period of their history. This people were also familiar with the use of emery powder, of talc applied to covering windows, and of rock crystal. We read in the translation of Abolais that crystal at that time was "found in many parts, albeit the the finest is that of Ethiopia. The substance which composes it is frozen water, petrified. And the proof of this is that when it is broken, small grains are discovered to be within, that made their entry as it was becoming stone (crystallizing); or again, in some of it is found what seems to be clear water. And it possesses two qualities in which it is distinct from every other stone : for when crystal is heated it receiveth any colouring that is applied to it, and is wrought with greater ease, besides being melted by fire ; insomuch that it can be made into any shape desired ; and if this shape be round, and the stone be set in the sun, it burneth anything inflammable that be set before it : yet does it not effect this by any virtue of its own, but by *the clearness of its substance,* and by the sunbeams which beat upon it, and by the roundness of its form."

We seem to foreshadow here, clearly enough, the application of this substance to making glasses to assist the sight, especially when the author of the treatise adds that on looking through the crystal, the human eye discovers "details of the greatest beauty, and things that are secreted from the simple (*i.e.* the unaided) vision."

Rico y Sinobas (who possessed a fine collection of antique glass, Spanish and non-Spanish) inclined to think that in the time of the Romans the finest and strongest glass, as well as the costliest and the most sought after, was that which was manufactured in Spain. In early times the chief centres of Spanish glass-making were situated in the heart of the Peninsula (where now is New Castile), in the neighbourhood of Tortosa, and in certain districts lying between the Pyrenees and the coast of Cataluña, though subsequently the practice of this craft extended through the kingdoms of Valencia and Murcia, and the valleys of Ollería, Salinas, Busot, and the Rio Almanzora, forming a zone which reached from Cape Creus to Cape Gata. Other regions in which the craft was introduced, apparently at a later epoch, were those of the Mediterranean littoral, Cuenca, Toledo, Avila, Segovia, and other parts of New Castile, as far as the slopes of the Sierra de Guadarrama. In the rest of the Peninsula there is not the slightest indication (excepting an obscure reference by Strabo, to vessels and receptacles of *wax*) that glass was made during the Roman domination of the country, either in Andalusia, Lusitania (Portugal), or in the northern regions of Cantabria.

Rico y Sinobas has described a Spanish glass-oven of those primitive times. He says that such as were used for making objects of a fair size consisted of three compartments resting one upon the other; the lowest cylindrical, to hold the fire and ashes, the next with a domed top, for concentrating the heat, and the third and uppermost, which also had a domed top, for holding the pieces of glass that were set to cool by slow degrees. The wall of the oven contained a number of openings, which served, according to the level at which they were situated, for controlling the fire, adjusting the crucibles, or extracting, by means of metal rods, the lumps of molten glass, previously to submitting them to the action of the blowpipe. The dimensions of

230

GLASS

such of these primitive ovens as have been found in Spain or Italy, are nine feet in height by six feet in diameter, and the material of which they are built is argil, of a kind insensible to heat, and carefully freed by washing from all foreign, soluble, or inflammable substances. The crucibles, which were fitted in the oven two, four, or at most six at a time, were of this argil also, wrought and purified with even greater care. Ovens and crucibles of a smaller size were used for making diminutive objects such as beads and imitation precious stones.[1]

Almería was probably the most important centre of Spanish-Moorish glass-making, and is mentioned in connection with this craft by Al-Makkari. The oriental shape of the older vessels which were made in this locality is still preserved in certain objects such as jars, bowls, flasks, and *aguardiente*-bottles, which are still manufactured, or were so until quite recently, throughout a region extending from Almería to the slopes of the Alpujarra. "All these objects," says Riaño, "are decorated with a serrated ornamentation of buttons, trellis-work, and the lines to which I have already

---

[1] Rico y Sinobas, *Del Vidrio y de sus artífices en España* (*Almanaque del Museo de la Industria*, 1870).

alluded, which were placed there after the object was made, in the Roman style. The paste is generally of a dark green colour, and when we find these same features in vessels of clear white glass, we may affirm that they are contemporary imitations made at Cadalso or elsewhere, for they are very seldom to be met with in the provinces of Almería and Granada, and are generally found at Toledo and other localities ; it is, moreover, a common condition of oriental art that its general form complies with a geometrical tracery, and we never find, as in Italian works of art, forms and capricious ornamentations which interfere with the symmetry of the general lines, and sacrifice them to the beauty of the whole."

None of the original Moorish glass of the Alhambra has survived till nowadays. Most of it was destroyed by the explosion, in the year 1590, of a powder factory which lay immediately beneath the palace and beside the river Darro. In the Alhambra archives, particular mention is made of the circular glass windows or "eyes," only the corresponding holes of which remain, in the baths of the same palace. This glass, which may have been in colour, was also destroyed by the explosion, as were the windows, "painted in colour with fancy devices and Arabic lettering," of the Sala de Embajadores,[1] those of the Hall of the Two Sisters, and certain windows, "painted with many histories and royal arms," belonging to the church of the Alhambra.

Excellent glass, reported by some authors to have equalled that of Venice, was made at Barcelona from as early as the thirteenth century. An inventory of the Crown of Aragon, dated A.D. 1389 and quoted by García Llansó, mentions as manufactured here, glass sweetmeat-vessels, cups, and silver-mounted tankards blazoned with the royal arms. The guild of Barcelona glassmakers was founded in 1455, and later in the same century Jerónimo Paulo wrote that "glass vessels of varying quality and shape, and which may well compete with the Venetian, are exported to Rome and other places." Similar statements are made by Marineus Siculus and Gaspar Barreyros.

Other centres of Spanish glass-making were Caspe in Aragon, Seville, Valencia,[2] Pinar de la

---

[1] Oliver, *Granada y sus monumentos árabes.*

[2] The inventory (A.D. 1560) of the Dukes of Alburquerque mentions "a white box with four small bottles of Valencia glass containing ointment for the hands." Other objects specified in this inventory are "a large glass cup, with two lizards for handles, and two more lizards on the cover"; "three glass cocoanuts, partly coloured

Vidriera, Royo Molino (near Jaen,) El Recuenco (Guadalajara), Cebreros (Avila), Medina del Campo, Venta del Cojo, Venta de los Toros de Guisando, and Castiel de la Peña in Castile. The glass-works of Castiel de la Peña were founded by the intelligent and indefatigable Hernando de Zafra, secretary to the Catholic sovereigns, Ferdinand and Isabella. "It has been calculated," says Riaño, "that about two tons of sand were used at these glass-works every month."

More important than the foregoing was the famous factory of a village in Toledo province called Cadalso, or sometimes, from the nature of its only industry, Cadalso (or Cadahalso) de los Vidrios. The glass made here is mentioned in terms of high praise by various writers of the sixteenth and seventeenth centuries, such as Marineus Siculus and Mendez Silva. The former of these authors says in his work upon the *Memorable Things of Spain*: "Glass was produced in several towns of Castile, the most important being that of Cadalso, which supplied the whole kingdom." Ewers and bottles of Cadalso glass and with gold blown into them, together with their covers "; and "a large glass cup, of Barcelona, blown with gold." The value of these cups, if they existed now, would not be less than two or three hundred pounds apiece.

LXXIV

VESSELS OF SPANISH GLASS
(South Kensington Museum)

are mentioned in the Alburquerque inventory. Mendez Silva says that the number of ovens was originally three, and that their coloured glass was equal to Venetian (Plate lxxiv.). This was towards the middle of the seventeenth century. Larruga tells us that by the end of the eighteenth this local industry was languishing. One of the three ovens had been abandoned. The other two produced inferior glass, as well as in diminished quantities.

The glass of Cataluña maintained its ancient reputation all through the fifteenth and sixteenth centuries and part of the seventeenth, and at this time was still compared with the Venetian by observant travellers (Plate lxxv.). Besides the capital, the principal glass-works in this province were at Almatret, Moncada, Cervelló, and Mataró. In 1489 a Barcelonese, by name Vicente Sala, and his sons applied to the City Council for leave to construct an oven at Moncada "in order to pursue the craft of glass-making, *lo qual a present aci se obre axi bellament e suptil com en part del mon* (seeing that the glass we manufacture in this neighbourhood competes with any in the world for subtlety and beauty)."

A document is extant from which we learn that

the City Councillors of Barcelona made strenuous efforts to prevail upon Ferdinand the Catholic to abolish a certain monopoly or other form of exclusive privilege which he had conceded to a local glass-maker. The result of this appeal is not recorded. In 1503 Ferdinand presented his consort with two hundred and seventy-four glass objects made at Barcelona, and Philip the Second possessed a hundred and nineteen pieces proceeding from the same locality.

An important development of this craft was the manufacture of coloured glass for churches and cathedrals. In the Peninsula, the earliest introducers of this branch of glass-making were principally natives of Germany, France, and Flanders, who came to Spain at the beginning of the fifteenth century.[1] Many of the oldest windows executed by these foreigners, or by the Spaniards who were taught by them, are still existing in the cathedrals of León, Toledo, Burgos, Barcelona,

---

[1] Before this time, however, Aymerich had written, in or about the year 1100, that sixty large windows in Santiago cathedral were closed by glass, which probably was coloured. We also hear of Francisco Socoma, who made or fitted windows of coloured glass at Palma, in the island of Majorca, in 1380, and of Guillermo de Collivella, who, in 1391, fitted at Lerida the glass which had been coloured for the cathedral of that town by Juan de San-Amat.

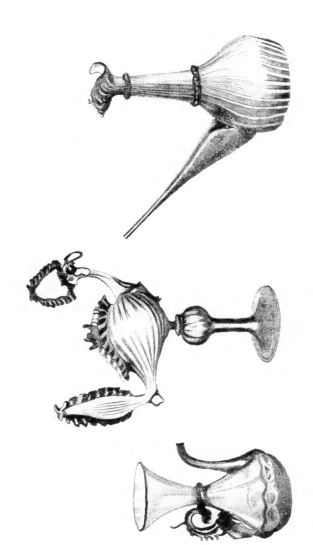

LXXV

VESSELS OF CATALAN GLASS

(From Drawings by the Author)

GLASS

and the Seo of Zaragoza. León has several
windows which date from as far back as the thirteenth century, and in which the glass is in small
pieces, arranged as though it were mosaic. Some
of the later and larger windows in the same
cathedral are thirty-five feet high, and one, dating
from the sixteenth century, is believed to have
been presented to this temple by Mary of
England, prior to her marriage with Philip the
Second.

It was, however, in the twelfth and thirteenth
centuries that the custom became general, in
Spain as in other lands, of colouring the surface
of white glass by partial fusing—a process which
is mentioned in the treatise of Abolais, to which I
have referred repeatedly. Between the eleventh
and the thirteenth centuries the coloured windows
of Spanish temples were still composed of pieces
of glass united in the manner of mosaic, forming
ornamental patterns of stars and similar devices ;
but subsequently to this period the decorative
themes are said to be painted *en caballete*, and
consist of figures, or the representation of scenes
from Scripture. In Spain, and dating from the
twelfth century, the workshops for preparing this
coloured glass were commonly situated within the

precincts of important temples, such as Toledo cathedral, or else, as was the case at Burgos, in separate buildings and *dependencias*. Here, in the square ovens characteristic of that age, and before it was mounted in the ponderous leaden frame, the glass was coloured with exquisite solicitude and patience by the hand of the master-craftsman, sometimes with a colour upon one of its surfaces alone, sometimes with the same colour upon both, or sometimes with a different colour upon either surface. The cartoons from which such windows were constructed, and which were often designed by painters of renown, were usually three in number. The first contained, upon a reduced scale, a coloured outline of the window; the second, drawn to the exact scale of the window as it was to be, was composed of all the pieces cut out and numbered according to the various colours; and the third, also of the projected size of the window, was kept complete, to serve as a pattern in case the window should suffer any accident, and require to be restored or mended. Not one of these cartoons is known to be preserved to-day, but Rico y Sinobas points out that from the strong and simple character of their colouring and outline, the illuminated illustrations

GLASS

of Spanish thirteenth century manuscripts, such as the *Cantigas*, and the *Book of Chess* of Alfonso the Learned, may well have been utilized for, or else be copied from, glass windows of that period.

As soon as the cartoon was finished, the window-painter traced it upon the surface of the glass. This was in square pieces, fitted conveniently together, with sufficient space between the pieces to allow the passage of the leads. Before being laid upon the glass and being submitted to the fixing action of fire, the colours were mixed with honey, urine, vinegar, and other fluids or substances which served as mediums to attach the colour to the glass. Thus prepared, and in the form of powder, the colours were allowed to dry for two or three days before the glass was placed in the oven. Yellow, which was the strongest colour, and that which penetrated deepest beneath the surface of the glass, was made from certain combinations of silver and nitrate of potash, while oxides or other forms of copper, lead, iron, tin, silver, and manganese, were used for making black, white, red, green, blue, purple, violet, or flesh-colour. These colours penetrated the glass to the depth of about half a millimetre ; but sometimes, after the colour had been applied, the craftsman would submit the glass to friction by a wooden polisher or wheel, thus giving it an appearance of greater clearness and transparency at any spot he might desire.

Among the artists who produced the coloured windows of León cathedral were Master Joan de Arge (A.D. 1424), Master Baldovín, and Rodrigo de Ferreras. Those of Toledo date from early in the fifteenth century, and were made by Albert of Holland, Vasco Troya, Luis Pedro Francés, Juan de Campos, and others, including the eminent Dolfín, who, according to Cean, began to work here in 1418, by order of the archbishop, Don Sancho de Rojas. The documents collected and published for the first time by Zarco del Valle tell us that on March 22nd, 1424, Dolfín received from Alfonso Martinez, treasurer and superintendent of works, two hundred gold florins and certain other moneys on account of his total payment of four hundred gold florins for "the eighth window he is making for the head of the cathedral." Other certificates of payment relating to Maestre Dolfín (as he always signed himself) are included in the same collection. By 1427 he was "defunct, God pardon him!" and the

GLASS

windows he had left unfinished were terminated by his assistant Lois (Louis).[1]

In 1458, and also at Toledo, a friar named Pablo began to repair the painted windows of the *crucero*. His pay was fixed by the "abbot and superintendent of works" at fifty *maravedis* each day, and that of "his lads, Ximeno and Juanico," at one half of this amount. Other artists engaged in the same work were Pablo (not the friar just referred to), Peter, a German, and "Master Henry," who was also German. Pablo received authority to purchase ten and a half *quintales* and thirteen pounds of coloured Flemish glass, at two thousand *maravedis* for each *quintal*. By a contract dated 1485 (he died between 1487 and 1493), Master Henry was handed by the cathedral authorities a sum of 150,000 *maravedis* "to proceed to Flanders or any other part he may desire, and where good glass is to be found, white, blue, green, scarlet, purple, yellow, or blackish (*prieto*), equal in thickness to the sample which he bears, and bring us thence such quantity as he has need of for the windows of our cathedral."

It is evident from this notice that Spain was

[1] *Documentos Inéditos para la Historia de las Bellas Artes en España*, p. 282 *et seq.*

then unable to produce the finest quality of glass. With such as he brought with him from abroad, Henry engaged to fashion "every kind of figure, image, scroll, and other object whatsoever be commanded him, according to the place it is to fill; the colours of the glass to be well mingled and distributed." He was also to make "the leaden casings stout and deep, so as to embrace and hold the glass aforesaid, that it may resist the air and wind." In return for this, he was to be supplied with an erected scaffolding, with all the chalk and iron he might require, and with the proper number of assistants, receiving, in payment of his labour, one hundred and fifteen *maravedis* for every square palm of glass the preparation of which should satisfy the superintendent and examiners of works.

One of the witnesses to this document was Henry's wife, María Maldonada, who came forward to affix her signature "with the license and pleasure of the aforesaid Master Enrique, her husband."

In 1433, Master Juan (perhaps the same as Joan de Arge, already mentioned) began to work at the windows of Burgos, where, later in this century, he was succeeded by Juan de Valdivieso and Diego de Santillana. We learn from the *Documentos Inéditos* (pp. 159, 160) that Santillana lived at Burgos, and that, on May 31st, 1512, he contracted to make three "historical windows" for the monastery of San Francisco, at a price of ninety-five *maravedis* for each palm of glass, this to be "of good colours and shades," and "measured by the Burgos standard." Two other contracts are preserved, signed by the same craftsman and both relating to Palencia. By one of them Santillana is to receive for six "storied windows," the subjects of which are specified, ninety-five *maravedis* the palm, besides the scaffolding and his house and coals.

Arnao de Flandes (Arnold of Flanders) was appointed master glass-painter to Burgos cathedral in 1512. Other glass-painters who worked here in the sixteenth century were Francisco de Valdivieso, Gaspar Cotin, Juan de Arce, his son Juan and grandson Pedro, and, in the seventeenth century, Valentin Ruiz, Francisco Alonso, Simon Ruiz, and Francisco Alcalde. Most of the windows made by all these men have been destroyed by time and weather, and have been replaced by barren panes of white; but a few fine specimens of the original work may yet be seen in the chapels of the Presentation, the Constable, and San Jerónimo. Perhaps the most remarkable of any is the rose-window above the Puerta del Sarmental.[1]

Other good cathedral windows prior to the sixteenth century are those of Avila, which date from about the year 1497, and were executed by Diego de Santillana, Juan de Valdivieso, and other artists ; those of the Seo of Zaragoza, by the Catalans Terri and Jayme Romeu (1447); and some at Barcelona, painted in 1494 by Gil Fontanet.

It is, however, in the sixteenth century that Spanish ecclesiastical window-glass attains its highest grade of excellence.[2]   Dating from this

---

[1] In the monastery of Miraflores, near this city, the queen of Ferdinand the Catholic built, at her expense, a rich pantheon to guard the ashes of her parents and her brother. The coloured glass was made by Simon of Cologne. One day, while visiting Miraflores, Isabella noticed upon the windows of this sanctuary the shield of a gentleman named Martin de Soria. Furious at the liberty thus taken with a fabric of her own, "afferte mihi gladium" she called in Latin to one of her attendants, and, raising the sword, dashed the offending window into a thousand pieces, crying that in that spot she would allow no arms but those of her father.

[2] Señor Lázaro, who has recently made at Madrid windows for León cathedral imitating those of the fourteenth and fifteenth centuries, remarks that with the sixteenth century the process grew more complicated, patterns composed with pieces of a single colour being replaced by glass containing a variety of tints. He has also discovered the following usage of the older Spanish craftsmen:

GLASS

century are windows in Toledo cathedral, painted in 1503 by Vasco de Troya, in 1509 by Alejo Jiménez, in 1513 by Gonzalo de Córdoba (these are considered by competent judges to be the finest of any), in 1515 by Juan de la Cuesta, in 1522 by Juan Campos, in 1525 by Albert of Holland, in 1534 by Juan de Ortega, and in 1542 by Nicolás Vergara the elder.[1] In 1537 Ortega was engaged to repair the damaged or broken panes at a yearly salary of 11,250 *maravedis*. Where the panes were wanting, he was to replace them by new ones painted by his hand, receiving, for each *palmo* of new glass so painted, an extra payment of ninety *maravedis*.[2]

In the same century the windows of Seville cathedral, begun some years previously (Cean says in 1504) by Micer Cristóbal Aleman ("Master

" By way of furnishing a key to their arrangement, all the pieces used to be marked with the point of a diamond, and this mark indicates the tone the glass requires for such and such a part of the design. The signs most often employed were three, namely X, L, and V, for red, blue and yellow respectively, intermediate tones being shown by combinations of these letters—XL, LV, XV, with "lines of unities" placed before or after to indicate the necessary gradation in the tone."

[1] This artist painted a series of magnificent windows representing scenes from the life of San Pedro Nolasco, for the convent of La Piedad, at Valencia.

[2] Zarco del Valle, *Documentos Inéditos, etc.*, pp. 339 *et seq.*

Christopher the German "), were continued by Masters Jacobo, Juan Juan Vivan, Juan Bernal, Bernardino de Gelandia, Juan Jaques, Arnold of Flanders (1525), Arnao de Vergara (1525), Charles of Bruges, (1557), and Vicente Menandro (1557).[1] In 1562 Diego de Valdivieso, and in 1570 Pedro de Valdivieso and Gerald of Holland, painted windows for Cuenca cathedral. In 1542 the same work was done at Palencia by Diego de Salcedo, and in 1533 George of Burgundy, "master in the art of glass," then resident at Burgos, proceeded to the same town and engaged

[1] According to Cean (*La Catedral de Sevilla*), Menandro painted in 1560 the conversion of Saint Paul on a window in the Chapel of Santiago, in 1567 another window with the scene of the Annunciation, over the gate of San Miguel, and in 1569 the companion to it, representing the Visitation, over the Puerta del Bautismo. "In all these windows," wrote Cean, prejudiced, as was customary in his day, in favour of the strictly classic style, "the drawing, pose, and composition are good, *although* in the draperies and figures we observe the influence of Germany."

In Cean's own time—that is, towards the close of the eighteenth century—the coloured windows of Seville Cathedral amounted to ninety-three, five of which were circular, and the rest with the pointed Gothic arch. The dimensions of the latter are twenty-eight feet high by twelve feet broad, and the subjects painted on them include the likenesses of prophets, patriarchs, martyrs, confessors, and virgins, or scenes from the New Testament, such as the rising of Lazarus, Christ driving the merchants from the temple, the Last Supper, and the anointing by Mary Magdalene.

to renew the cathedral windows at a cost of a hundred *maravedis* for every palm of coloured glass, and fifty for every palm of plain.[1]

In 1544, sixty-two windows in the nave of Segovia cathedral were filled with painted glass prepared chiefly at Valladolid and Medina del Campo, though some was brought from Flanders. The remaining windows were left unfilled till 1676, in which year a canon of the cathedral, named Tomás de la Plaza Aguirre, succeeded in rediscovering a formula for the practise of this craft, and the panes yet needed were made and coloured at Valdequemada by Juan Danis, under Plaza Aguirre's supervision. Thirty-three additional windows were completed from this factory. According to Lecea y García, the chapter of Segovia cathedral possess, or possessed for many years, two curious manuscripts relating severally to *The painting of glass windows*, by Francisco Herranz, and *Glass-making*, by Juan Danis—the same who owned and worked the factory at Valdequemada. These interesting treatises were examined by Bosarte, who has described them. He says that the one on glass-making consisted of twenty-three sheets of clear writing, and the

---

[1] Zarco del Valle, *Documentos Inéditos*, p. 159

one on glass-painting of eight sheets ; both manuscripts being in quarto size. The latter contained, distributed beside the text, sketches of the various instruments required for this craft. The other and longer monograph consisted of the following chapters : — (1) How to draw upon glass. (2) How to cut glass. (3) How to paint and shade glass. (4) Of the substances and ingredients for painting glass. (5) How to give a flesh-colour to glass. (6) How to give a yellow or golden colour to white or pale blue glass, but no other. (7) How to fire glass. (8) How to make the glass-oven.

Windows were painted in the cathedral of Palma de Mallorca by Sebastián Danglés in 1566 and by Juan Jordá in 1599, in that of Málaga by Octavio Valerio in 1579, and in those of Tarragona and Avila respectively, by Juan Guasch in 1571, and by Pierre de Chiberri in 1549. This craftsman was undoubtedly a foreigner. The following entry which concerns him is quoted by Rosell de Torres from the *Libro de Fábrica* of Segovia cathedral : " By order of the Canon Juan Rodriguez, on the twelfth day of August, I paid to Pierre de Chiberri, master-maker of window-glass, the sum of 56,560 *maravedis*, 34,960 for the casings of seven large windows with their side-windows—in all twenty-one casings—besides ten casings for the windows of the lower chapels, containing altogether MMMCCCCXCVI palms, amounting at ten *maravedis* the palm to the aforesaid 34,960 *maravedis*: also 19,125 *maravedis* for CCCLXXII palms of glass for the said chapels at a *real* and a half each palm, plus 2476 *maravedis* for certain glass which had yet to be measured because it was in the skylights. The total sum amounts to the aforesaid 56,560 *maravedis*." [1]

During the seventeenth century, glass-work of various kinds continued to be produced upon a large scale at Barcelona, Mataró, Gerona, Cuenca, Toledo, Valmaqueda, and Seville. In 1680 the Duke of Villahermosa established a glass factory at San Martin de Valdeiglesias, and placed it under the direction of a native of Namur named Diodonet Lambot, aided by various other artists from the Netherlands. In 1683 Lambot was succeeded by Santiago Vandoleto, who proved incompetent, and caused, in 1692, the total stoppage of the factory.

I have said that glass was made at Medina del

---

[1] Isidoro Rosell de Torres, *Las Vidrieras pintadas en España* (published in the *Museo Español de Antigüedades*).

Campo, in the province of Valladolid. Pinheiro da Veiga's *Pincigraphia*, written at the beginning of the seventeenth century, contains an interesting notice of this glassware. " Really, the glass-work of Valladolid is most beautiful, and worth going to see if only for the pleasure of its contemplation. There are objects of considerable size, such as (glass) pitchers of every form and colour. Others are called *penados*, and are of a syphon shape, pouring out water in small quantities.[1] Besides this there are all manner of cunningly contrived retorts such as we never see in Lisbon, and yet in Valladolid their cost is only moderate. . . . The principal shops for selling these and porcelain are two in number, and the prices are the same as in Portugal."

Two very important Spanish glass factories were founded in the eighteenth century. The first, which was under Crown protection, was established by Don Juan Goyeneche in the year 1720 at a place called Nuevo Baztán, in the province of Toledo. The royal privilege allowed this factory to produce "all articles of glass up to

---

[1] "*Penado.* A narrow-mouthed vessel that affords the liquor with scantiness and difficulty." Connelly and Higgins' Dictionary ; A.D. 1798.

a height of twenty inches, working and polishing the same, embellishing, and coating them with metal ; to make looking-glasses and similar orna-ments, glass vessels of all descriptions, white glass for window-panes, and glass objects of any kind or shape, whether already known to us, or that may be invented in the future."

The factory of Nuevo Baztán continued work-ing for some years, and turned out excellent glass for exportation to America and other parts ; but it was killed eventually by the rising price of fuel, and above all by competition from abroad. "When the foreigners," says Larruga in his *Memorias políticas y económicas*, "saw that the factory was in full swing, they conspired to bring about its ruin, and begged their ambassadors to communicate against it with the ministers ; but finding this of no avail, and recognising the importance to themselves of overthrowing this manufacture, they decided to sell glassware at a price at which it would be impossible to sell the products of Nuevo Baztán. The amount of this reduction was the one-third part of the entire value. By this means the foreigners made it impossible for the factory to support itself, since the objects it produced were laid away and found

no purchaser for years. This, and the cost of
the wood required to keep the ovens burning day
and night, not excepting feast-days (for to stop
the fires for a moment would have meant the
spoiling of the oven), induced the downfall of this
celebrated factory, as soon as the fuel of all the
neighbouring forests had been consumed."

Nevertheless, upon the closing of these works,
one of the experts who had been employed there,
a Catalan named Ventura Sit, attracted by the
forests of Valsain and the excellent and abundant
sand obtainable in this locality—principally from
near the villages of Espirdo and Bernuy de
Porreros—decided to open another glass-works at
La Granja. Here is the royal summer residence
of San Ildefonso, and Sit was fortunate enough to
secure at the outset—that is, in 1728—the firm
protection of Philip the Fifth and of his consort,
Isabel Farnese. Instructed by the sovereigns to
make some mirrors, he produced these objects of
a moderate size at first, increasing it, after the
year 1734, to a maximum length of 145 inches by
85 in breadth. Larruga says that these mirrors
were the largest produced anywhere at that time,
and they continued to be made until very nearly
the end of the century. They are often referred

to in the narratives of travellers. Swinburne wrote in 1776: "Not far from Carthagena is a place called Almazaron, where they gather a fine red earth called Almagra, used in the manufactures of Saint Ildephonso, for polishing looking-glasses. In Seville, it is worked up with the tobacco, to give it a colour, fix its volatility, and communicate to it that softness which constitutes the principal merit of Spanish snuff."

Describing the royal palace at Madrid, the same author says that the walls of the great audience-chamber "are incrustated with beautiful marble, and all round hung with large plates of looking-glass in rich frames. The manufactory of glass is at Saint Ildefonso, where they cast them of a very great size; but I am told they are apt to turn out much rougher and more full of flaws than those of France."

According to Townsend (1786), "The glass manufacture is here carried to a degree of perfection unknown in England. The largest mirrors are made in a brass frame, one hundred and sixty-two inches long, ninety-three wide, and six deep, weighing near nine tons. These are designed wholly for the royal palaces, and for presents from the king. Yet even for such purposes the factory is ill-placed, and proves a devouring monster in a country where provisions are dear, fuel scarce, and carriage exceedingly expensive."

Laborde wrote of the same factory a few years later : " There is also a glass-house, in which bottles are wrought of a superior quality ; and white glasses, which are carved with much ingenuity (Plates lxxvi. and lxxvii.). Near this glass-house has been founded a manufactory for mirrors, in a large and well-arranged edifice. There are two furnaces, and a considerable number of stoves, in which the plates are left to cool after they have been precipitated. They are of all dimensions, and the largest that have yet been fabricated. They are sometimes from a hundred, a hundred and thirty, or a hundred and thirty-five inches in height, to fifty, sixty, or sixty-five inches in breadth : they are expanded in the hand. The process for polishing them is performed by a machine ;[1] they are then transported to Madrid, for the purpose of being metallised It is not uncommon to see tables of bronze, on which mirrors are extended, a hundred and sixty inches in length, and ninety in breadth."

These tables are described by Bowles : " The largest measures a hundred and forty-five inches

[1] This machine was invented by a Catalan named Pedro Fronvila.

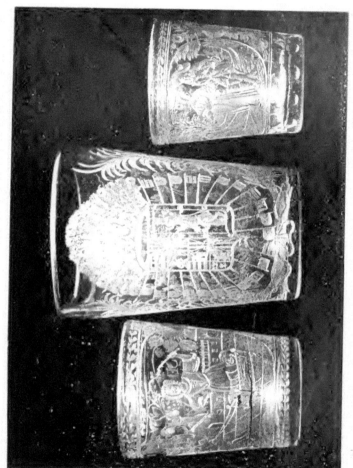

in length by eighty-five in breadth, and weighs
four hundred and five *arrobas*. The smallest
measures a hundred and twenty inches in length,
and seventy-five in breadth, and weighs three
hundred and eighty *arrobas*."

The best account of any is contained in the
Nouveau Voyage en Espagne (1789) of Bourgoing. This author wrote : "A côté de cette
Fabrique naissante de première necessité " (*i.e.*
the royal linen factory at La Granja) "il y en a
une de luxe qui remonte au regne de Philippe V ;
c'est une Manufacture de glaces, la seule qu'il
y ait en Espagne. On s'étoit d'abord borné à
une Verrerie qui subsiste encore, et donne des
bouteilles d'une assez bonne qualité, et des verres
blancs qu'on y cisele avec assez d'adresse. J'en
ai rapporté quelques-uns où l'on a gravé des chiffres,
des lettres, et jusqu'à de jolis paysages. Cette
Verrerie étoit un acheminement à une entreprise
plus brillante. La Manufacture de glaces de
Saint Ildephonse est comparable aux plus beaux
établissements de ce genre ; on en peut voir les
dessins dans les Planches de l'Encyclopédie.
L'édifice est vaste et très bien distribué ; il contient
deux fourneaux et une vingtaine de fours où l'on
fait refroidir lentement les glaces après les avoir

coulées. On y en coule dans toutes les dimensions depuis les carreaux de vitres jusqu'aux plus
grands trumeaux. Elles sont moins blanches
et peut-être moins bien polies que celles de Venise
et de St-Gobin ; mais nulle part on n'en a encore
coulé d'aussi grandes. L'opération du coulage s'y
fait avec beaucoup de précision et d'ensemble.
Monseigneur Comte d'Artois eut la curiosité d'y
assister ; la glace qu'on y coula devant lui avoit,
autant que je puis m'en souvenir, cent trente-trois
pouces de long, sur soixante-cinq de large, et l'on
m'a assuré qu'il y en avoit encore de plus grandes.
On les dégrossit à mains d'hommes dans une longue
galerie qui est attenante à la Fabrique, et il y a à
un quart de lieue une machine que l'eau fait mou-
voir, et où on acheve de les polir ; on les porte
ensuite à Madrid pour les étamer. Le Roi con-
sacre les plus belles à la parure de ses appartements ; il en fait des cadeaux aux Cours qui ont
des relations intimes avec lui. En 1783, S.M.C. en
fit joindre quelques-unes aux présens qu'il envoyoit
à la Porte Ottomane, avec laquelle elle venoit de
conclure un traité. C'est une idée agréable pour un
cosmopolite tolérant, de penser qu'en dépit des
préjugés de religion et de politique qui divisoient
autrefois les Nations, la main des arts a établi

GLASS

entr'elles un échange de jouissances d'un bout de l'Europe à l'autre, et que les beautés du serrail se mirent dans les glaces coulées à Saint-Ildefonse, tandis que les tapis de Turquie sont foulés par des pieds François. Ce qui sort d'ailleurs de la Manufacture de Saint-Ildefonse est vendu, pour le compte du Roi, à Madrid et dans les provinces ; mais on sent bien que ce profit est trop mince pour couvrir les frais d'un établissement aussi considérable qui, le bois excepté, est éloigné de toutes les matières premières qu'il employe, qui est situé fort avant dans l'intérieur des terres, au sein des montagnes, et loin de toute rivière navigable ; aussi doit il être compté parmi ces fondations de luxe qui prosperent à l'ombre du Trône, et qui ajoutent à son éclat." [1]

A few more details are added by Swinburne : " Below the town is the manufactory of plate-glass belonging to the crown, carried on under the direction of Mr Dowling ; two hundred and eighty men are employed. The largest plate they have made is one hundred and twenty-six Spanish inches long ; the small pieces are sold in looking-glasses all over the kingdom ; but I am told the king makes no great profit by it ; however, it is

[1] Vol. I., pp. 144-147.

a very material point to be able to supply his
subjects with a good commodity, and to keep in
the country a large sum of money that heretofore
went out annually to purchase it from strangers.
They also make bottles and drinking-glasses
(Plates lxxvi., lxxvii.) ; and are now busy erecting
very spacious new furnaces to enlarge the works.
To provide fuel for the fires, they have put the
pinewoods under proper regulations and stated
falls ; twenty-seven mule-loads of fir-wood are
consumed every day ; and four loads cost the king,
including all the expenses of cutting and bringing
down from the mountains, about forty reals."

In 1736, the first factory which had been
established at San Ildefonso was nearly destroyed
by fire ; but the damage was repaired, and the
factory placed under state control. Its finances
were at no time prosperous. In 1762 Charles the
Third granted a privilege reserving to it the
exclusive sale of glass within a radius of twenty
leagues from Madrid and Segovia ; but the sales
did not improve. In spite of this, the monarch,
a few years later, erected a new and costly
factory from designs by Villanueva and Real.
There were two departments in this ample
building. One, for the manufacture of the

LXXVII

GLASS OF THE FACTORY OF SAN ILDEFONSO

GLASS

plainest glass, was directed by a Hanoverian, named Sigismund Brun; and the other, devoted to smaller and more elaborate articles, by Eder, a Swede. "The greater number of the objects made at these important works were of transparent, colourless glass, possessing a marked French style, and were either richly engraved and cut, or gilded, or sometimes (though less often) they were made of coloured and enamelled glass. At this time, too, were manufactured mirrors for the royal palaces, as well as candlesticks and chandeliers of great beauty, following the Venetian method, and embellished with coloured flowers."[1]

In spite of all these efforts, the works at the dawn of the nineteenth century were in a moribund condition. In 1829 they passed into the hands

[1] Breñosa and Castellarnau; *Guide to San Ildefonso* (1884), p. 53. Rico y Sinobas observes that in the objects produced at the factory of La Granja, the glass itself is inferior to the engraving or cutting with which it is adorned. This leads him to infer that the foreigners brought over by the kings of Spain to superintend the factory, were cutters and engravers of glass, rather than skilled glass-makers. He also draws attention to the fact that the Spanish monarchs chose these foreign craftsmen from too limited a class, entrusting the most important posts at all the royal factories to Frenchmen who were stated to descend from the old nobility of their native country. In this manner the progress and welfare of the craft itself was sacrificed to an insane prejudice in favour of the aristocratic origin of the craftsman.

of private persons, who also failed to make them pay, and subsequently, owing to the ineptitude of Spanish governments and the severity of foreign competition, have definitely closed their doors.

" In Catalonia," wrote Laborde, towards the year 1800, "are two glass houses; but the glass blown in them is dark, and destitute of lustre. Aragon has four, one at Alfamen, one at Peñalva, one at Utrillas, and one at Jaulin, which is the largest; but the quality of the glass is not superior to that of Catalonia. The glass-house at Utrillas produces both flint and common glass. Glass houses are also established at Pajarejo and at Recuenco in Castile, which manufacture the most beautifully white and transparent glass."

In 1791 there were six glass-ovens in the kingdom of Valencia, situated at Valencia, Alicante, Salines, Olleria, and Alcira. They turned out 2100 pieces in this year, some of which were exported to Castile and Aragon.[1]

Early in the eighteenth century the glass of Barcelona was praised by Alvarez de Colmenar (" Il s'y fait de belles verreries "), and we know

---

[1] Ricord; *Noticia de las varias y diferentes Producciones del Reyno de Valencia, etc.: segun el estado que tenian en el año* 1791. Valencia, 1793.

that all through this period her *forns de vidre* continued to produce good work, including holy-water vessels of uncoloured glass relieved with blue or with the fine white *latticinio*, the local *arruixadors* or *borrachas*, and the typical *porrón*. The former of these vessels is of small size, and has several spouts. Commonly it is filled with scented water for gallants to sprinkle on girls at dances in the public square. The *porrón* invariably excites the curiosity of foreigners,[1] and is often thought to be of purely Spanish origin. This is not so. Upon a Roman lampstand in Naples museum is a figure of Bacchus riding on a tiger and "holding in his hand the horn from which the ancients drank, using it as, among some other peoples, do the modern Catalans—that is, not placing the vessel in their mouth, but holding it aloft and thus imbibing it; a method which requires no small amount of practice." In fact, there is reason to believe that the *porrón* is derived from a similar vessel in use among the ancient

---

[1] "The mode of drinking in this country is singular; they hold a broad-bottom'd glass bottle at arm's length, and let the liquor spout out of a long neck upon their tongue; from what I see, their expertness at this exercise arises from frequent practise; for the Catalans drink often and in large quantities, but as yet I have not seen any of them intoxicated."—Swinburne.

Persians, who poured their liquor from it into the hollow of the hand, and thence imbibed it in the fashion called, in Cataluña and Valencia, *al gallet*. For just as a certain class of American displays his marksmanship in spitting, so does the Catalan who is accomplished in the art, amuse himself and others by causing the ruby wine to spout from his *porrón* on to the very apex of his nose, continuing from this point, in the form of a fine and undulating rivulet, over his upper lip and down his throat.

Windows of Spanish houses were seldom glazed until about one hundred years ago. When Bertaut de Rouen travelled here in 1659, this fact impressed him disagreeably. Even in the royal palace at Madrid he found that there were chambers "qui n'ont point du tout de fenestrés, ou qui n'en ont qu'une petite, et d'où le jour ne vient que d'enhaut, le verre estant fort rare en Espagne, et la pluspart des fenestrés des maisons n'ayant pas de vitres." In 1787, Arthur Young was no less horrified at the glassless condition of the houses in Cataluña. "Reach Sulló; the inn so bad that our guide would not permit us to enter it, so he went to the house of the Curé. A scene followed so new to English eyes, that we could not refrain from laughing very heartily. Not a pane of glass in the whole town, but our reverend host had a chimney in his kitchen; he ran to the river to catch trout; a man brought us some chickens which were put to death on the spot. . . . This town and its inhabitants are, to the eye, equally wretched, the smoke-holes instead of chimneys, the total want of glass windows—the cheerfulness of which, to the eye, is known only by the want."

However, as an exception to this doleful rule, the town of Poeblar had "some good houses with glass windows, and we saw a well-dressed young lady gallanted by two monks."

PRINTED BY
NEILL AND COMPANY, LIMITED,
EDINBURGH.

Lightning Source UK Ltd.
Milton Keynes UK
UKHW011120140620
364911UK00004B/871